# Concise Historical Atlas of World War Two

# CONCISE HISTORICAL ATLAS OF WORLD WAR TWO
## THE GEOGRAPHY OF CONFLICT

RONALD STORY
University of Massachusetts Amherst

New York ■ Oxford
OXFORD UNIVERSITY PRESS
2006

Oxford University Press, Inc., publishes works that further Oxford University's
objective of excellence in research, scholarship, and education.

Oxford   New York
Auckland   Cape Town   Dar es SalaamHong KongKarachi
Kuala Lumpur   MadridMelbourne   Mexico City   Nairobi
New Delhi   ShanghaiTaipei   Toronto

With offices in
Argentina   Austria   Brazil   Chile   Czech Republic   France   Greece
Guatemala   Hungary   Italy   JapanPolandPortugal   Singapore
South Korea   SwitzerlandThailand   Turkey   UkraineVietnam

Published by Oxford University Press, Inc.
198 Madison Avenue, New York, New York 10016
http://www.oup.com

Oxford is a registered trademark of Oxford University Press

**Library of Congress Cataloging-in-Publication Data**

Concise historical atlas of World War Two / by Ronald Story.
    p. cm.
    Includes index.
    ISBN 13: 978-0-19-518219-4 (cloth)—ISBN 13: 978-0-19-518220-0 (pbk.)
1. World War, 1939-1945—Campaigns—Maps. 2. Historical geography—Maps. I.
    Story, Ronald.

G1038.H52 2005
940.54'022'3—dc22

                                                        2004632269

Printing number: 9 8 7 6 5 4

Printed in Hong Kong
on acid-free paper

# TABLE OF CONTENTS

# Concise Historical Atlas of World War Two

# INTRODUCTION

## MAPS AND WAR

Students of history need maps. The essence of history is movement over time and space. Maps help show that movement. This is especially true for the study of war. Maps help illustrate the geopolitics of war—the dynamics of expansion and the forging of alliances—as well as the disposition of military forces. The physical features of maps—mountain ranges, forests, rivers, shorelines, oceans, marshes, deserts—help explain why forces move along certain trajectories rather than others, why battles develop in this way rather than that way, why campaigns result in absolute or partial or Pyrrhic victories. Political boundaries, including shifting boundaries over time, help reveal the motives for expansion, the search for allies, the cost to populations and governments, the subsequent reconfigurations of power.

Maps in and of themselves do not by any means explain everything. It was not inevitable that the United States would send troops in the 19th century to smash the armies of the Confederacy or in the early 20th century to fight Imperial Germany. Those actions reflected the exercise of political will. Geography, however, was a factor in the decision making of Abraham Lincoln and Woodrow Wilson, just as it was in the initial decisions of Jefferson Davis and Kaiser Wilhelm to provoke war. Geography, moreover, helped determine how U.S. troops would later advance—down the river valleys of the South or into the accessible terrain of Northern France.

World War Two, perhaps more than any other war, requires maps for full comprehension. The reasons for this include at least the following:

**a.** The participation of countries with far-flung colonies and dominions in Asia, Africa, the Pacific, and the Western Hemisphere. These countries (the United States, Great Britain, France, the Netherlands) drew on the resources of their possessions and dominions to wage war. Equally important, they fought to hold and recapture them. Understanding this war, therefore, requires some knowledge of the geography of the globe—of Puerto Rico and Newfoundland as well as Algeria and South Africa, India and the East Indies, New Guinea and the Marianas.

**b.** The vaulting ambitions of the Axis Powers (Germany, Italy, Japan), all of which sought to conquer and either exploit or absorb extensive new territories in Europe, the Mediterranean, and Asia. Understanding these vast, initially successful thrusts requires maps.

**c.** The immensity and relative unfamiliarity (to Western readers) of the Soviet Union, a vital partner in the fabled Grand Alliance that defeated the Axis. Much of the fighting and suffering of World War Two took place on Soviet soil. Understanding the movement of German armies on the Russian Front and the resistance and countermovement of the Red Army, and why the former ultimately failed and the latter succeeded, requires maps.

**d.** The immensity and relative unfamiliarity (to Western readers) of China, the scene of early Western exploitation and nearly as much wartime suffering as the U.S.S.R. Here Imperial Japan deployed 2 million troops. Here Nationalists and Communists began the bloody civil war that would shape the fate of the postwar world. The contours of this crucial part of the war are impossible to comprehend without maps.

**e.** The immense naval operations of the war, stemming largely from the facts that two major combatants, Britain and Japan, were island maritime powers and that another, the United States, had to project its force across large oceans. Connecting the coasts of every inhabited continent, the world's sea-lanes were points of vulnerability, magnets for submarine attacks, routes for military aid and invasion buildups, and pathways for the amphibious operations that swept Japan from the Pacific. Maps make all this clearer.

**f.** The full harnessing to military purposes of the power of the internal combustion engine, which enabled ground forces to plunge rapidly into enemy territory while aircraft attacked enemy forces (including civilians) hundreds and even thousands of miles away. Thus arose modern "lightning" armored warfare and high-altitude strategic bombing, both of which expanded the battlefield and the campaign theater and changed the nature of combat. Mapping motorized attacks and bombing runs is therefore vital to our understanding of this war.

**g.** The extraordinary number of famous and climactic battles: France and the Battle of Britain, El Alamein and Stalingrad, Normandy and Kursk, Malaya and the Philippines, Midway, Iwo Jima and Okinawa. All receive their due here, as do some that are less well known—White Russia, Berlin, and the Marianas, among others. So, too, do the devastation of Hiroshima and Dresden and the sprawling network of Axis concentration, labor, slave, and death camps.

The maps in this book, then, offer a view of movement, especially military movement, in space. They also offer a view of movement over time. Most historians think of the war in Europe as beginning with the German invasion of Poland in 1939, which is duly illustrated here. But there was much background to this attack and to the European war generally. Map 1 shows the disposition of forces in 1914 to indicate how the contending alliances in World War One resembled but differed from those of World War Two and also, by virtue of relief features, suggests why the armies in both wars moved along similar paths. Map 2 shows Africa in 1914, heavily colonized and therefore a likely field of competition and conflict in the 1930s and 1940s.

Along these lines, most historians think of the war in Asia and the Pacific as beginning with the seizure of Manchuria, if not the attack on Pearl Harbor. Here, however, the first Asia-Pacific maps show the pattern of early Western colonialism in Asia and the humiliation of China at Western and Japanese—and Russian—hands, background not only for the Japanese offensives against China but for the Chinese civil war. The final maps for both Europe and Asia illustrate the reconfiguration of post-Nazi Europe and the sweeping decolonization of the postwar era, products of World War Two.

The book should serve well as a supplement to fuller accounts, and as a desk and reserve reference for serious students, in a concise format that would leave time to explore other topics: ideology, industrial production, popular culture, scientific developments, demography, art, literature, religion, postwar philosophy, the raising and supplying of armies, the experience of combat, women, children, refugees, life in the camps, secret police, occupation, and the war's towering military and political personalities, to mention only a few.

Taken together, however, the 50 maps and their commentaries in this volume do offer a succinct, serviceable overview of the coming, prosecution, and consequences of World War Two. One of the virtues of seeing a war through maps is that the maps tell the story to some degree by themselves. With enough good maps and reasonable explanatory texts—readers will presumably find both here—the basic contours of the war come through.


## TERMS

Military historians use certain terms on the assumption that students will know them, which is not always the case. A few words of explanation might be of value.

**Division.** A large, more or less self-contained military formation. In World War Two divisions constituted the main measure of combat strength. Most divisions were infantry divisions composed mainly of riflemen. There were also cavalry, airborne, artillery and, increasingly in all forces, tank (armored) divisions. Peak-strength divisions in World War Two numbered about 15,000 men organized into three regiments or brigades, plus attached medical, communications, police, artillery, tank and other elements. Chinese divisions were smaller, as were German divisions late in the war. Japanese and U.S. Marine divisions were significantly larger.

**Formation.** Anything from a regiment or brigade on up. A *corps* consisted of two or more divisions, an *army* had two or more corps, an *army group* was two or more armies. Thus Erwin Rommel's force in North Africa was the Africa Corps because it contained two armored divisions; each German army group in the U.S.S.R. would have contained at least eight divisions. A Soviet *front* was the equivalent of an army group. *Units* were, in general, any element smaller than a brigade or regiment—a battalion, a company, and a squad or section.

**Wehrmacht.** The German armed forces. *Luftwaffe* was the German air force; *Kriegsmarine* was the German navy. *Blitzkrieg* was rapidly moving mechanized and armored warfare.

**Armor.** Tanks or self-propelled guns. Both had tracks rather than wheels and thick protective steel plating. A tank had a rotating gun turret, which the self-propelled guns did not. Germany called its tanks *panzers* and deployed them, along with trucks and other motor vehicles, in mounting blitzkrieg, the "lightning" war that overwhelmed Poland and France. Mechanized or motorized formations, including tanks, trucks, motorcycles, and cars, moved at the speed of the internal combustion engine rather than the speed of a walking soldier or horse.

**Salient.** A major protrusion in the front line. Commanders were ever alert for the development of a salient, which could be either exploited by the offense to achieve a breakthrough or pinched off by the defense via attacks against its flanks and the subsequent isolation and annihilation of the protruding force. Commanders commonly tried to keep their front lines straight to avoid this kind of pinching flank attack. At Kursk in 1943, the German attempt to pinch off the great Soviet salient failed, with dramatic consequences.

**Flank.** The side of an enemy position or column. It was harder to defend a flank attack than a frontal assault because the defenses on the side of a position were usually less well prepared, and it was also harder to bring maximum firepower to bear against an attacker. Rapidly moving columns of motorized forces were particularly vulnerable to flank attacks, which could cut essential supply lines. The Germans slowed their armored attack through Northern France in 1940 partly because they feared a flank attack against their panzer columns.

**Combined arms.** The simultaneous application of infantry, artillery, armored divisions, and air forces against an enemy. The Germans first perfected this technique, but others, especially the

United States, eventually followed suit. *Close air support,* a crucial dimension of combined arms and a particular hallmark of German combat, indicated the use of air power in support of ground operations. Its antithesis was *strategic bombing,* a hallmark of British and U.S. air operations. *Amphibious warfare* was a version of combined arms that incorporated sea power with the other components to capture shore and island positions by assault from the sea. This became a U.S. Navy and Marine specialty in World War Two, although the British, Japanese, Russian, and U.S. Armies relied on it as well.

## NUMBERS

Students of World War Two quickly learn that combatant, casualty, and death figures vary widely. This is partly because of the high rates of desertion in some military forces, partly because of carelessness in distinguishing total casualties from total dead, partly because of the immense civilian casualties in some theaters, partly because post-war governments sometimes obscured total casualties, partly because of the difficulty of determining what constituted a casualty of war per se as opposed to a casualty of industrial production, colonial brutality, civil strife, or crime against humanity.

Estimates of total dead vary, for example, from 35,000 to 250,000 at Nanking; from 10,000 to 125,000 at Dresden; from 50,000 to 300,000 at Hiroshima. Estimates of Soviet war dead range from 20 million to, in recent studies, over 30 million; and of Chinese dead, from 6 million to 12 million. Three million people died in India during the war from famine and famine-related disease. Some historians number these among the war dead because the British military had commandeered the railways, which were therefore unavailable to distribute grain to stricken regions; others argue that famine was common in India and should not be charged to the war. The Chinese numbers are contentious for the same reason, and also because many records were lost during the civil war, which itself killed hundreds of thousands. In the United States, some 400,000 workers died or were injured each year in industrial accidents; some of this may be attributed to the grueling pace of war production, but not all, so it is unclear whether to count these as war casualties.

The figures used in this book are best estimates drawn from recent scholarship. In most cases they are rounded to make it easier for students to compare and remember them.

## HELPFUL BOOKS

Among the thousands of fine studies of World War Two, the following proved especially useful in the crafting of the maps and commentaries for this volume:

Robert Abzug, *Inside the Vicious Heart*
Stephen Ambrose, *Citizen Soldiers*
John Barber and Mark Harrison, *The Soviet Home Front*
W. G. Beasley, *The Rise of Modern Japan*
Herbert Bix, *Hirohito and the Making of Modern Japan*
Michael Burleigh, *The Third Reich*
Peter Calvocoressi, Guy Wint, and John Pritchard, *The Penguin History of the Second World War*

John Costello, *The Pacific War*

I. C. B. Dear and M. R. D. Foot, eds., *The Oxford Companion to World War II*

John Dower, *Embracing Defeat*

Edward L. Dreyer, *China at War*

J. F. Dunnigan et al., *War in the East: The Russo-German Conflict*

John Erickson, *The Road to Berlin*

George Feiffer, *Tennozan*

Richard Frank, *Downfall*

Martin Gilbert, *The Second World War*

Meiron Harries and Susie Harries, *Soldiers of the Sun*

Eisei Ishikawa and David Swain (trans.), *Hiroshima and Nagasaki*

Julian Jackson, *The Fall of France*

John Keegan, *Six Armies in Normandy* and *The Second World War*

Domingue Lormier, *Les Combats Victorieux*

William Manchester, *Goodbye, Darkness*

Henri Michel, *The Second World War*

Nathan Miller, *War at Sea*

Williamson Murray and Allan R. Millett, *A War to Be Won*

Richard Overy, *Russia's War* and, with Andrew Wheatcroft, *The Road to War*

Stephen Pelz, *Race to Pearl Harbor*

Anthony Read and David Fisher, *The Fall of Berlin*

Alan Sharp, *The Versailles Settlement*

W. R. Smyser, *From Yalta to Berlin*

George Stein, *The Waffen SS*

Warren Tute, John Costello, and Terry Hughes, *D-Day*

H. P. Willmott, *The Second World War in the Far East*

Robert Young, *France and the Origins of the Second World War*

Thomas Zeiler, *Unconditional Defeat*

## Acknowledgments

A number of people at OUP made valuable contributions to this work. My thanks to Peter Coveney, my former editor; June Kim, assistant editor; Elyse Dubin, director of editing, design, and production; Lisa Grzan, production editor; and Annika Sarin, designer. My thanks also to John Challice, vice president and publisher, for the special attention he gave this project in its later stages. I would also like to thank Oxford's seven outside readers: James C. Bradford of Texas A&M University; Joseph Dawson of Texas A&M University; Marvin Fletcher of Ohio University; William L. O'Neill of Rutgers, State University of New Jersey; Mark Parillo of Kansas State University; Donald Shaffer of University of Northern Colorado; and Thomas Zeiler of University of Colorado.

For a century European statesmen preserved the peace through shifting alliances designed to maintain a balance of power that would discourage aggression. The system worked as long as statesmen were restrained, armies were small, and no one country became too powerful. Russia, France, and Britain expanded via colonial conquests in Asia and Africa. New states such as Italy and Germany concentrated mainly on building themselves. European wars were quick and limited.

Two new factors threatened this system. One was the growth of Imperial Germany. Unified in 1871 following the seizure of Alsace and Lorraine from France, the German population grew more rapidly than that of its neighbors, as did its economy, whose output of steel, chemicals, heavy machinery, and other basic commodities made it a rival to Britain and the United States and superior to everyone else. Moreover, Germany's autocratic Kaiser Wilhelm had expansionist ambitions and was willing to draw on not only a modern economy but a proud military tradition to achieve them.

A second threat was the rise of a fervent nationalism that corresponded to ethnic and language groups rather than state boundaries and was therefore both divisive and expansionist. On the one hand, various minorities (Serbs, Czechs, Poles, Arabs) worked to throw off the yoke of Tsarist Russians, Ottoman Turks, and especially the Austro-Hungarian Monarchy, thereby threatening to fragment these states. On the other hand, extreme nationalists (pan-Germans, pan-Slavs) wanted their entire group somehow together. This would require rearranging the frontiers of Europe, which would mean war.

Thus arose the alliances of the Great War. Austria-Hungary, large but not strong, moved against nationalist insurrection in the Balkans. Russia, seeing fellow Slavs under attack, mobilized to defend them. Germany, the single strongest country, sided with the Austrians. Since Britain and France were increasingly partners with Russia in containing German power, the Germans invaded France in hopes of winning a quick victory in the west so that they could turn unmolested to the east and avoid a two-front war. Italy soon joined the Russians in opposing its competitor, Austria.

The Germans expected to win through mass mobilization: equipping millions of men with millions of tons of artillery, machine guns, food, and other supplies, all carried to the front by rail under the planning of a meticulous general staff. They would attack, moreover, through the flat lands of the Low Countries and Poland, areas well suited by topography for the swift advance of armies. But the French and British, too, mobilized mass armies with mass-produced modern weaponry so that the Germans—whose troops, dumped by rail at the front, still moved unprotected at the speed of walking men and horses—faltered in the teeth of the same kind of artillery and machine guns that they themselves carried. The French and British also had to advance slowly and unprotected, and they also faltered. Lacking radio communications or, until late in the war, aerial observation, neither central command could counterpunch effectively. Everywhere, soldiers dug into the earth to escape the storm of fire, steel, and lead.

The result was years of murderous trench warfare. The Germans were more successful in the east, where the Tsarist armies proved monstrously inept. But without a victory in the west, German hopes were dashed, and U.S. entry into the war in 1917 on the Anglo-French side brought not only soldiers but an economic prowess that Germany, weakened by a British naval blockade, could not match. Armistice came in 1918—too late to save the collapsing monarchies of Austria-Hungary, Russia, Turkey, and Germany or the lives of 10 million soldiers and several million civilians. The war that broke out 20 years later resembled this one in many respects. It also differed dramatically, not least in all but reversing this ratio of military to civilian dead.

# N

## ATLANTIC OCEAN

| | |
|---|---|
| Central Powers | |
| Allied Powers | |
| Neutral countries | |

IRELAND

GREAT BRITAIN

NORTH Sea

NORWAY

SWEDEN

DENMARK

NETH.

BEL.

LUX.

LORRAINE

ALSACE

SWITZ.

FRANCE

SPAIN

PORTUGAL

SP. MOROCCO

MOROCCO (FR.)

ALGERIA (FR.)

TUNISIA (FR.)

Corsica

Sardinia

Sicily

Mediterranean Sea

Baltic Sea

FINLAND

ESTONIA

LIVONIA

KURLAND

LITHUANIA

EAST PRUSSIA

POLAND

GERMANY

AUSTRIA-HUNGARY

RUSSIA

UKRAINE

RUMANIA

SERBIA

MONTENEGRO

ALBANIA

BULGARIA

GREECE

Sarajevo

ITALY

Black Sea

TURKEY

Cyprus

Crete

500 Miles

500 Kilometers

0

0

# 2 AFRICA

Explored and exploited since the Renaissance, Africa by 1914 was the most heavily colonized area of the world and a long-standing focus of European competition, a situation that remained true even after the Versailles Treaty stripped a defeated Germany of its colonial possessions.

The dominant power in Africa was Great Britain, which controlled a corridor stretching from its protectorate, Egypt, all the way to its dominion, the Union of South Africa, except for a German claim near Lake Victoria that Versailles awarded, along with Southwest Africa, to Britain, thus completing the British corridor. There were more British colonies in West Africa, including Nigeria and especially Sierra Leone, a staging area for convoys.

British control of its eastern African corridor was important for strategic as well as economic reasons. Italy's conquest of Ethiopia in 1935–1936, for example, imperiled the Red Sea shipping lanes to the Arabian Peninsula and the Far East and therefore access to India and Malaya. Clearing Axis forces from the Horn of Africa was thus a high British priority when war broke out. The Fascist advance from Libya toward the Suez Canal, the linchpin of the entire British Empire, prompted an even more vigorous response. Britain labored politically to retain the loyalty of South Africa, which both commanded the shipping lanes around the Cape of Good Hope and contained a large Afrikaner population with German sympathies. British troops wrested the big island of Madagascar from collaborationist Vichy France in 1942 for a similar reason—to dissuade Japan from extending its naval presence to the coast of Africa and thereby keep the Axis powers away from an essential supply line to the Desert Army in Egypt.

The second colonial power in Africa was France, which controlled the bulk of West Africa from Algeria and the Muslim North to the Atlantic colonies of Mauritania, Guinea, and the Ivory Coast. French authority resumed in Equatorial Africa, including (after 1919) the ex-German colony of Kamerun (Cameroun). After the defeat of France in 1940, Hitler allowed his Vichy satellite to control the French colonies, an indirect arrangement that Charles de Gaulle later exploited to build support among colonial administrators and garrisons for Free France.

Of the other powers, Portugal, whose colonies in southern Africa were strategically situated, remained neutral despite the Axis sympathies of dictator Antonio Salazar, largely to keep the Royal Navy from shelling its cities. The Spanish dictator, Francisco Franco, drew support from Spain's African colonies in seizing power in the 1930s. But Franco, too, refused to join the Axis powers formally, so his possessions, though close to Gibraltar, played little part in the fighting—much to the relief of the Allied troops who landed in Algeria and Morocco in late 1942. Germany never accessed the mineral resources of the Congo even after overrunning Belgium in 1940.

In a sense the Nazis made control by the traditional European powers easier by fixing their racism on Jews and Slavs rather than Africans and Asians and by colonizing to the east rather than the south. Italy was different, but Italy was weak. Black African units served Britain and France with distinction during the war. Most black Africans, however, showed no interest in choosing sides in a war between white Europeans. After all, Britain and France had failed to help one of only two independent African countries, Ethiopia, when Italy invaded in 1935. That failure was not forgotten.

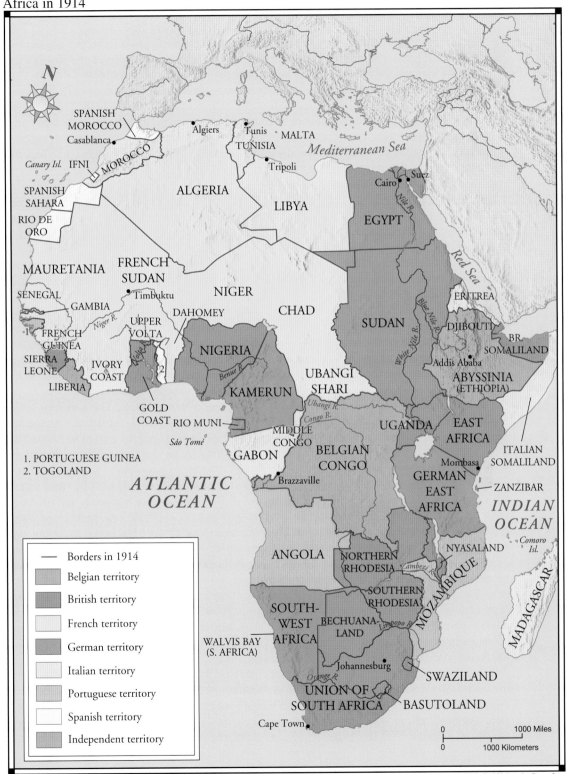

N

SPANISH
MOROCCO
Casablanca

Algiers

Tunis
TUNISIA

MALTA

*Mediterranean Sea*

Tripoli

Cairo • Suez

*Canary Isl.* IFNI
MOROCCO

SPANISH
SAHARA

RIO DE
ORO

MAURETANIA

FRENCH
SUDAN

Timbuktu

ALGERIA

LIBYA

EGYPT

*Nile R.*

*Red Sea*

NIGER

CHAD

SUDAN

ERITREA

DJIBOUTI

BR.
SOMALILAND

SENEGAL

GAMBIA

DAHOMEY

*Niger R.*

UPPER
VOLTA

FRENCH
GUINEA

SIERRA
LEONE

LIBERIA

IVORY
COAST

GOLD
COAST

NIGERIA

*Benue R.*

KAMERUN

UBANGI
SHARI

*Blue Nile R.*

*White Nile R.*

Addis Ababa

ABYSSINIA
(ETHIOPIA)

UGANDA

EAST
AFRICA

*Ubangi R.*

*Congo R.*

ITALIAN
SOMALILAND

RIO MUNI

*São Tomé*

GABON

MIDDLE
CONGO

Brazzaville

BELGIAN
CONGO

Mombasa

GERMAN
EAST
AFRICA

ZANZIBAR

*INDIAN
OCEAN*

1. PORTUGUESE GUINEA
2. TOGOLAND

*ATLANTIC
OCEAN*

ANGOLA

NORTHERN
RHODESIA

*Zambezi R.*

NYASALAND

*Comoro
Isl.*

MOZAMBIQUE

MADAGASCAR

SOUTHERN
RHODESIA

— Borders in 1914

Belgian territory

British territory

French territory

German territory

Italian territory

Portuguese territory

Spanish territory

Independent territory

SOUTH-
WEST
AFRICA

WALVIS BAY
(S. AFRICA)

BECHUANA-
LAND

*Limpopo R.*

SWAZILAND

Johannesburg

UNION OF
SOUTH AFRICA

BASUTOLAND

*Orange R.*

Cape Town

0          1000 Miles

0       1000 Kilometers

© Oxford University Press, Inc.

9

# 3 EUROPE IN 1920

The 1919 peace conference led by France, Britain, and the United States faced two urgent challenges: to fill the yawning East European vacuum left by the collapse of the Russian and Austro-Hungarian monarchies and to deal with a defeated Germany and its empire.

The East European question was particularly pressing. Conditions were chaotic. There seemed no hope of resurrecting either an alternative polyglot empire or a regional federation. Bolshevism seemed likely to spread. Given the clamor of countless ethnic groups and Woodrow Wilson's support for self-determination, it was perhaps inevitable that the peacemakers would seek to establish independent states roughly matching the ethnic, religious, and linguistic groups and then hope for the best.

Thus arose a chief consequence of World War One: a string of new countries stretching from the Baltic to the Adriatic. First came (top of the map) Finland, Estonia, Latvia, and Lithuania, all detached from Russia; then came Poland, enlarged with slices of Russian and German territory, and Czechoslovakia, a linguistic hodgepodge. Then there were Hungary and Austria, shrunk and split apart, and Yugoslavia, encompassing bitter ethnic and religious factions. Of the preexisting states, Rumania was enlarged at Russian and Hungarian expense; Bulgaria, Albania, and Greece lost little except their ambitions. Ottoman Turkey meanwhile seethed with the indignity of defeat and the loss of land to France and Britain, the Middle East's new masters, and was therefore ripe for revolution in 1922.

There were some unhappy truths about these states, including the nine new ones. First, they were mostly small and riven by ethnic conflict. Second, they were poor, with only pockets of manufacturing. Third, they resented and feared one another, precluding military collaboration. Hungary, Austria, and Bulgaria, all ex-German allies, felt abused and alienated from the peace process. It is difficult to see what else the peacemakers might have done. Nevertheless, the whole region would be vulnerable to powerful "revisionist" predators, should any someday arise.

Germany, now a parliamentary democracy, was a longer-term problem. The territorial settlements seemed modest at the time. All its overseas colonies went, mostly to Britain. Alsace and Lorraine reverted to France, as expected, and part of East Prussia went to Poland to provide the Poles with a harbor. German-speaking western Czechoslovakia, known as the Sudetenland, stayed there despite German pleas.

The victors also wrote a "war guilt" clause into the peace treaty and imposed financial reparations on the Germans to pay both for the destruction of Belgian and French industry and for Allied soldiers' pensions. The French, desperate for fuel, got to work the Saar coal mines, just inside Germany, subject to an eventual plebiscite. The Rhineland, which France had hoped to control, was to remain free of German troops. Union with Austria, which wanted to join Germany, was forbidden.

Some of these provisions reflected French fear of future German aggression, as did provisions restricting the German military: no conscription or general staff; no submarines, battleships, tanks, or air force; and a standing army of only 100,000. But restrictions have to be policed, and Germany, beaten but not occupied or broken up, was still by far the most powerful country economically and demographically in Europe, as it had been in 1914. Nor was the fear misplaced. Stinging from defeat and having a proud military heritage, the Germans found the war guilt clause, the reparations, the Polish corridor, and the army restrictions hateful.

Only with British help could France do the policing, but Britain would agree to help only if the United States would also agree. Woodrow Wilson hoped to resolve some of these difficulties through the League of Nations, whose charter would bind member states to combine to halt aggression. But the American Senate rejected membership in the League. Britain therefore declined a formal French alliance. With the Anglo-Americans unreliable and Russia under the hated Bolsheviks, France turned, inevitably but unwisely, to the only apparent alternative—the new countries of Eastern Europe.

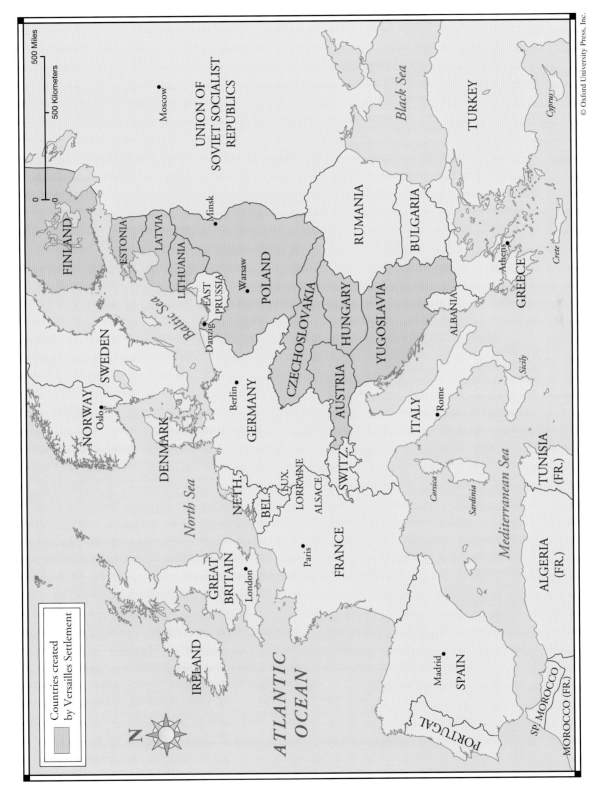

# 4 THE FRENCH FRONTIER BETWEEN THE WORLD WARS

France in the 1920s had two military goals: to find allies against a possible resurgent Germany and to avoid the astronomical casualties and territorial devastation that the Germans had inflicted in the Great War if war did come.

Absent full participation by the United States and the Soviet Union (U.S.S.R.) and the reluctance of Britain to ally formally, France looked for allies first in Italy, where years of diplomatic overtures produced almost nothing, and then in Eastern Europe, where several new states—Poland, Czechoslovakia, Rumania, Yugoslavia—owed their existence to the French-influenced peace settlement and were likely partners (though inherently weak ones) against aggression. France signed treaties with them all. In the 1925 Treaty of Locarno, France, Germany, Italy, and Britain pledged to respect the existing national boundaries. The pledge had no teeth but hopefully reflected genuine sentiments.

Ultimately, most French understood that without a British alliance, France would have to stand largely alone, as was evident from the Versailles Treaty itself, which provided for a demilitarized Rhineland, the industrial sector on either side of the Rhine River. This would make it hard for Germany to defend the area and easy for France to occupy it, which happened briefly in the mid-1920s. Germany without the Rhineland would not have the resources to wage a long war; with it, France could. Even if the worst happened, German armies would have to advance farther before reaching France, giving the French more time to mobilize.

But to occupy the Rhineland would mean not only high occupation costs and German aggravation but a kind of preemptive aggression that the French, like everyone else, were loathe to undertake. Moreover, the French desperately wanted to avoid fighting a slogging, murderous infantry and artillery war of the 1914–1918 variety. One option was to modernize the army in the interest of rapid mobility and the quick strike, thus taking the fight to the enemy. But France had an existing arsenal left over from the Great War and was reluctant to pour vast sums into a modernization campaign, especially since German intentions seemed, in the 1920s, peaceful.

Instead, beginning in 1929, France erected the world's largest system of fixed fortifications, the Maginot Line. The strongest forts stretched from the Belgian border past the Saar coal region to the point where the Rhine turned southward; lesser defenses proceeded to the Swiss frontier and down to the coast. The Maginot Line was an engineering marvel that would almost certainly have withstood sustained enemy assault. Its limits were that it constituted a static defense when armies were becoming more mobile and, worse, that it stopped at the Belgian border. Belgium was in fact a glaring weakness. Shattered in World War One, the Belgians hoped to remain neutral next time and so refused to permit an extension of the Maginot Line into their territory. This partly thwarted the intent of the line, which was to keep the next war away from French soil and factories. Even so, for all its enormous cost, the Maginot Line seemed the right move, at least in the 1920s when Europe appeared disposed to peace.

By the mid-1930s things had changed. Adoph Hitler, the bellicose new chancellor of Germany, was pledging to reverse the 1919 settlement and restore German greatness. In 1936 he sent troops into the Rhineland, upending this safeguard. Neither France nor Britain contested him. Yet despite the onset of the Great Depression, successive French governments began the slow process of force modernization, including more aircraft and armored vehicles, and this modernization would accelerate after Germany absorbed Austria and Czechoslovakia in 1938. The Maginot Line and Hitler's peace protestations notwithstanding, France girded itself to move into Belgium to confront advancing German armies.

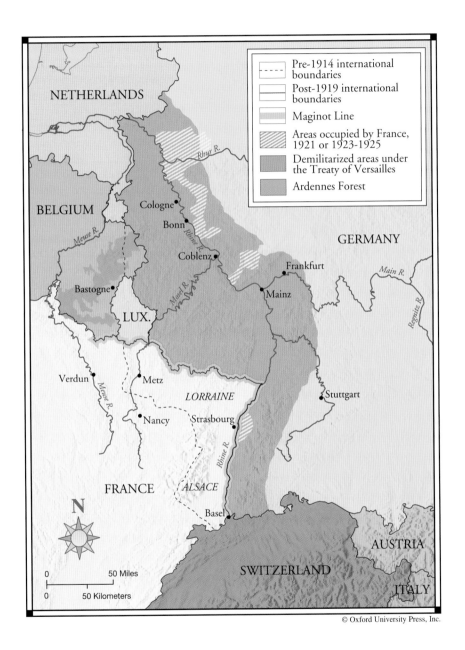

NETHERLANDS

BELGIUM

GERMANY

Cologne

Bonn

Coblenz

Frankfurt

Mainz

Bastogne

LUX.

Verdun

Metz

Stuttgart

LORRAINE

Nancy

Strasbourg

FRANCE

ALSACE

Basel

AUSTRIA

SWITZERLAND

ITALY

*Rhyr R.*

*Meuse R.*

*Rhine R.*

*Musel R.*

*Main R.*

*Regnitz R.*

*Meuse R.*

*Rhine R.*

N

0        50 Miles

0        50 Kilometers

Pre-1914 international
boundaries

Post-1919 international
boundaries

Maginot Line

Areas occupied by France,
1921 or 1923-1925

Demilitarized areas under
the Treaty of Versailles

Ardennes Forest

© Oxford University Press, Inc.

# 5    SPAIN

In July 1936, only months after Fascist Italy invaded Ethiopia and Germany reoccupied the Rhineland, a group of Spanish army officers, backed by the Catholic Church and the great landowners, called for troops to support them in overthrowing the left-leaning constitutional government of Spain. Their stated aim was to prevent a Communist takeover and halt the spread of peasant unrest and labor agitation. Thus began the third of the so-called prewar European crises, a civil war that would last three years, kill or wound nearly a million people, and offer the first indication that perhaps the next war would be ideologically and technologically different from the last.

The right-wing "Nationalist" call to arms was only partially successful. Garrisons in the southwest of the country joined them, as did most of the northwest. But the Basque region around the industrial city of Bilbao in the far north, Barcelona and its Catalonian hinterlands near the French frontier, and a populous triangle stretching from the capital of Madrid to Valencia on the Mediterranean to Granada in the far south all remained loyal to the elected government. In late July General Francisco Franco, a Nationalist leader in Spanish Morocco, asked Hitler for help and got it: transport planes to ferry Spanish colonial troops to Spain to strengthen the insurgent garrisons. Franco, emerging as the undisputed Nationalist leader, now joined forces with the Falange, Spain's fascist movement. Germany reinforced him with the Wehrmacht's Condor Legion, including tanks and combat planes. Fascist Italy, seeing a kindred spirit, sent equipment and 70,000 soldiers.

The Republican "Loyalists" countered with foreign assistance of their own. Since France, Britain, and the United States all declared neutrality and refused to support the Republic, help came chiefly in two forms: tanks, planes, and military advisors from the Soviet Union and the International Brigades, 35,000 liberal, Marxist, and Jewish volunteers from across Europe and North America willing to battle the forces of fascist aggression. But the Loyalists were playing a weak hand. Catalonians and Basques resisted central authority; workers and peasants divided their allegiances among constitutionalists, socialists, Communists, and (a Spanish specialty) anarchists, all having different goals and none trusting the others. The Russians seldom spoke Spanish; the International Brigaders were ill-trained and ill-equipped.

By October 1937 Franco's Nationalists had subdued the Basques, won the west and most of the south, and fought their way to the outskirts of Madrid and Catalonia. Here the Loyalists held, but they did not have the troops, supplies, or leadership to counterattack. The Brigaders departed in late 1938; four months later the Nationalist army entered Madrid, inaugurating a dictatorship that lasted until Franco's death in 1975.

Franco's triumph represented an extension of right-wing influence to the western Mediterranean and still more pressure on France, which now had hostile governments on three sides instead of two. Equally important, the war showcased both the bitter ideological passions of the 1930s, which transcended frontiers and allegiances, and the new modes of warfare, which included rapid armor movement and the bombing and strafing of civilian targets, as when the Germans annihilated the village of Guernica, a horror depicted by the Spanish artist Picasso in World War Two's best known work of art.

Dedicated to the crusade against Marxism and liberalism, Franco joined the Anti-Comintern Pact with Germany, Italy, and Japan; sold iron ore to Germany on favorable terms; and contributed an army division to the invasion of the U.S.S.R. in 1941. But Spain, horribly poor and with massive losses from the civil war, was in no shape to do more. Franco therefore remained neutral in World War Two, meaning German troops could not cross Spain to attack the British at Gibraltar.

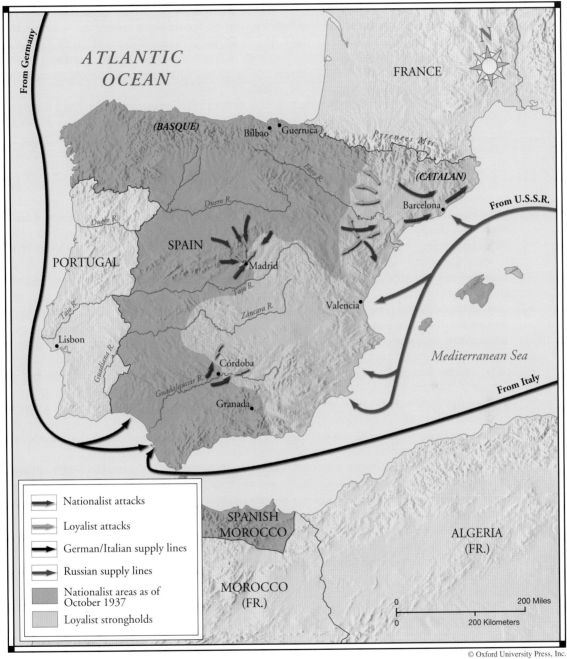

ATLANTIC
OCEAN

FRANCE

From Germany

*(BASQUE)*

Bilbao  Guernica

*Pyrenees Mts.*

*(CATALAN)*

Barcelona

From U.S.S.R.

*Ebro R.*

*Duero R.*

SPAIN

*Duero R.*

PORTUGAL

Madrid

*Tajo R.*

*Záncara R.*

Valencia

*Mediterranean Sea*

*Tajo R.*

Lisbon

*Guadiana R.*

Córdoba

*Guadalquivir R.*

Granada

From Italy

N

| | Nationalist attacks |
| | Loyalist attacks |
| | German/Italian supply lines |
| | Russian supply lines |
| | Nationalist areas as of October 1937 |
| | Loyalist strongholds |

SPANISH
MOROCCO

ALGERIA
(FR.)

MOROCCO
(FR.)

| 0 | | 200 Miles |
| 0 | | 200 Kilometers |

Adolph Hitler's immediate concern upon becoming chancellor in 1933 was to achieve absolute internal authority, which he quickly did through ruling by emergency decree, abolishing labor unions and non-Nazi parties, controlling the media, imprisoning opponents, murdering rivals. He replaced or arrested independent-minded military officials. Soldiers now saluted the Nazi flag and swore allegiance to Hitler personally rather than to Germany. Acting from strength, he instituted conscription, revealed the existence of the Luftwaffe, began building battleships, and doubled (and then doubled again) the army budget. He sent troops into the Rhineland in 1936 partly because he needed the region's industry for his military buildup.

But Hitler had other goals as well. One was to "purify" Germany through harsh measures against Jews, the infamous Nuremberg Laws of 1935. Another move, also racial, was to absorb all Germans into a new Reich (empire), where they belonged according to what Hitler claimed was the "natural law" of race solidarity. Thus ensued the last of the great prewar crises after the events in Ethiopia, Spain, and the Rhineland—the overrunning of Austria and Czechoslovakia.

Austria possessed many assets: a population of 7 million ethnic Germans, productive farmland, timber and iron ore, gold reserves. At Versailles the Austrians had asked for *Anchluss* (unification with Germany), a request the French and Italians rejected. In the early 1930s, the Austrian Nazi party, with Hitler's covert support, revived the demand, which was only narrowly averted when Mussolini, fearing too much German power, sent troops to the border. But by 1938 Italy was busy in Spain and Africa, and France was increasingly defensive. So when Hitler and the local Nazis again insisted that "the same blood belongs in a common Reich," there was no counterweight. Hitler threatened invasion. The Austrian chancellor resigned, handing power to the Nazis, and German troops poured across the border; Hitler proclaimed Austria a Reich province. A wave of terror targeted Jews, socialists, even Catholics. Thousands fled to Switzerland and Czechoslovakia before the borders were shut down.

Besides gold, resources, and people, Austria offered advantages that leap from the map: control of the Danube transportation system, the highway to the Balkans, and a strategic position against the southern Czech frontier—a "lower jaw," in Len Deighton's vivid phrase, with which to crush Czechoslovakia. Czechoslovakia differed from Austria. It had twice as many people, only a minority of whom were ethnic Germans. It had a functioning parliamentary democracy and significant industry, including the great Skoda factories, which produced some of the better tanks and artillery on the continent. Its mountainous western frontier was well defended with big guns.

But Czechoslovakia contained seven mutually suspicious ethnic groups, and its German minority, in the Sudetenland near the Reich itself, was under the sway of local Nazis, who wielded the weapons of propaganda and street violence to demand special privileges and (eventually, in accord with Hitler's wishes) the protection of the Third Reich. France and Britain, having failed to prevent *Anchluss* in Austria despite the provisions of Versailles, were reluctant to see Germany gain still more power. But they were not yet ready for war despite the various treaties and the possibility that Czechoslovakia, unlike Austria, could defend itself, and in a series of September meetings culminating at Munich, they forced Prague to give up the Sudetenland. Hitler pledged to seek no new land.

In fact, Hitler had vast ambitions and was spoiling for war, as he informed his generals in May. He therefore made new demands on Czechoslovakia. Seeing little sign of help and now without their mountain defenses, the Czechs signed a treaty turning their country into a German protectorate; the German army entered Prague in March 1939. Adolph Hitler had not only his German population but a strategic advantage—a frontier extending toward the hated Soviets and, more immediately, a position on the southern Polish border, another "lower jaw," this time with which to crush Poland.

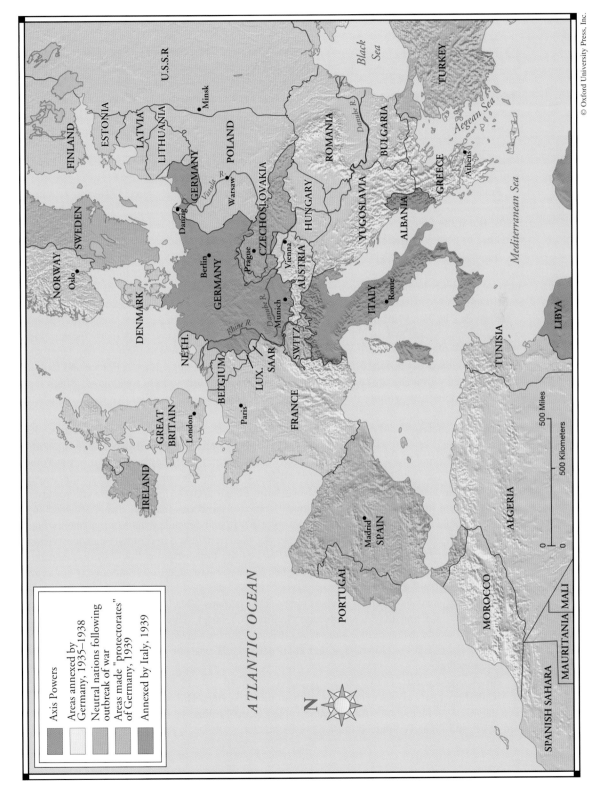

© Oxford University Press, Inc.

**Axis Powers**

Areas annexed by
Germany, 1935–1938

Neutral nations following
outbreak of war

Areas made "protectorates"
of Germany, 1939

Annexed by Italy, 1939

*ATLANTIC OCEAN*

N

IRELAND

GREAT
BRITAIN

London

NETH.

BELGIUM

LUX.

FRANCE

Paris

SAAR

SWITZ.

GERMANY

Berlin

Munich

*Rhine R.*

*Danube R.*

AUSTRIA

Vienna

Prague

CZECHOSLOVAKIA

Danzig

*Vistula R.*

Warsaw

POLAND

GERMANY

LITHUANIA

LATVIA

ESTONIA

FINLAND

SWEDEN

NORWAY

Oslo

DENMARK

U.S.S.R

Minsk

HUNGARY

*Danube R.*

ROMANIA

YUGOSLAVIA

ALBANIA

BULGARIA

GREECE

Athens

*Aegean Sea*

TURKEY

*Black Sea*

ITALY

Rome

*Mediterranean Sea*

LIBYA

TUNISIA

ALGERIA

MOROCCO

SPAIN

Madrid

PORTUGAL

SPANISH SAHARA

MAURITANIA

MALI

500 Miles

500 Kilometers

0

0

# 7 THE INVASION OF POLAND

Post-Versailles Poland was a country of some 24 million, larger than Austria and Czechoslovakia combined and roughly equal in population and area to Spain at the opposite corner of Europe, which it resembled in its Catholic conservatism, agrarian economy, and dreams of past glory. But where the Pyrenees isolated Spain and protected it against invasion, Poland's frontiers were flat, offering access to European markets and culture but making it easy to invade, as both Germans and Russians had done repeatedly and recently. Whereas Spain was ethnically unified, Poland was only 75 percent Polish; the rest was Russian or Ukrainian in the east or German in the west. The Polish Corridor (including the port of Danzig) not only was heavily German but separated East Prussia from the Fatherland, a source of tension that Hitler eagerly exploited.

Poland had beaten the Red Army during the Russian civil wars after 1918 and remained impressive enough to motivate France (though not Britain) to sign a mutual defense treaty in the 1920s. But if the Poles detested Germany, they detested Russia even more and so rejected French entreaties to permit Soviet troops into Poland if Germany attacked.

By mid-1939 Hitler, deprived of war in Czechoslovakia, was committed to one in Poland. Despite the Franco-Polish treaty and the growing alarm in London, he did not think the West would interfere, particularly after he signed a startling nonaggression and trade pact with Premier Joseph Stalin that included a secret protocol allowing the Soviets to occupy eastern Poland in case of war.

Even so, the Poles did not altogether despair. They believed that France and Britain would eventually respond and that the Polish army could withstand the Wehrmacht for many months, long enough for the West to mobilize and confront Hitler with what he feared most—a two-front war. This proved only partly accurate. When the Germans attacked on September 1, France and Britain, after issuing an ultimatum, did declare war. But they intended less to fight for Poland, which they considered indefensible without Russian involvement, than to signal to Hitler that they would fight him at some point.

The Poles moreover did not hold out, largely because the Germans fought a war that emphasized surprise and velocity as well as firepower. German armies attacked at dawn from the north, west, and south while Stuka dive bombers and Messerschmitt fighters destroyed most of the Polish air force, disrupted mobilization, and bombed Warsaw, a full hundred miles from the border. Rapidly moving German infantry isolated one large Polish army at the western frontier and cut another to pieces in the Corridor with an attack from two directions that had strong armored support. Heinz Guderian's XIX Panzerkorps, the world's first independent tank army, then swung 200 miles southeastward to attack the Polish reserves. Guderian linked in turn with panzer divisions from Army Group South to encircle what remained of the Polish troops. Soviet forces occupied eastern Poland; Warsaw capitulated on September 27. A war expected to last months, if not years, was over in less than four weeks.

The Germans attacked with 1 million men versus perhaps 600,000 mobilized Poles and used twice the firepower, but they won because they moved faster. This was not quite the modern blitzkrieg that would defeat France and savage Russia—horses were more common than trucks, the tanks were light, and envelopment rather than penetration was the rule—but it was ruthlessly dazzling nonetheless.

The Germans totaled 14,000 dead and 30,000 wounded, but Poland lost 1 million men (including 800,000 prisoners of war), a quarter of them to the Soviets. Hitler loathed the Poles and dealt more harshly with them than with any other subject people (other than Russians). He loathed Jews even more, and Poland contained millions of them.

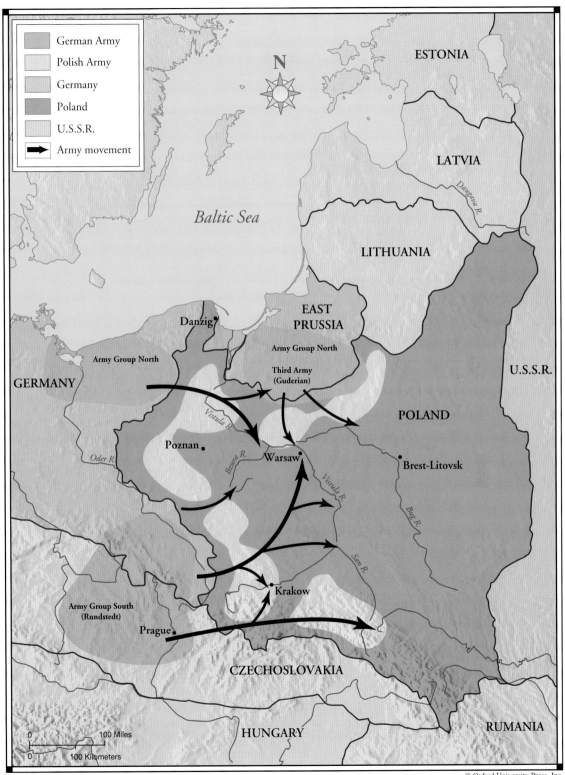

# 8 THE FALL OF FRANCE

Germany's pattern of occupation and conquest formed an expanding concentric circle: Austria, Czechoslovakia, Poland. Hitler, it was assumed, would soon expand the circle to the Low Countries and France, which he did. But first, in order to keep Britain away from his flank and his supplies of Swedish iron ore and to ensure access to the North Atlantic, he expanded it to Scandinavia. Denmark fell to tank units, Norway to airborne troops and naval assault. The Kriegsmarine (German navy) lost several surface vessels to Oslo and Royal Navy gunners, but the Germans beat back ill-planned British and French landings on the Norwegian coast. The U.S.S.R. meanwhile subdued Finland, a former Russian possession.

German Army Group B attacked Holland, which had hoped to remain neutral, on May 10 with 29 divisions. The Germans landed troops in seaplanes on the Rotterdam canals, seized bridges with troops wearing Dutch uniforms, and threatened to bomb the city to ruins unless the Dutch surrendered. Surrender came, (although not soon enough to keep all the bombs away). German troops next sped into Belgium (where the great fortress of Eben Emael fell to Wehrmacht forces in gliders) to confront the Allied forces, who had swung northward, as anticipated, to meet the invasion. The fighting went badly for the Allies, partly because Belgium, professing neutrality, had not prepared proper defenses and partly because frightened civilians clogged the roads and prevented the movement of soldiers and supplies.

But the main reason for the Allied difficulties was that Germany had changed its invasion plan from one of massive weight against Belgium and northern France, as in 1914, to a powerful armored thrust through Luxembourg's Ardennes forest just west of the Maginot Line. The French had only the weak Ninth Army there because they considered the forest unpassable. So did the Germans until early 1940, when Heinz Guderian, a leading tank proponent and a hero of the Polish campaign, argued that tanks and trucks with air support could get through the Ardennes and, once through, could drive to the English Channel, sever Allied communications and transportation, and seal off the British Expeditionary Force (BEF) and the French Seventh and First Armies. The idea excited Hitler, and Army Group A found itself with 44 divisions, including nearly all the panzer divisions.

Hitler's excitement was well grounded. The panzers, with close air support, hit the hinge, or "elbow," of the Allied line at the Meuse River with maximum force. On May 13 the 7$^{th}$ Panzer Division of General Erwin Rommel reached the river near Dinant. Two days later, thanks to hard fighting and Rommel's leadership, the tanks were across and rolling westward; by May 17 the division had captured 10,000 soldiers and 100 enemy tanks and had driven a 60-mile wedge into the defenses. By May 14 Guderian's tank corps was also across and moving west; a day later all seven tank divisions were across. Fast-moving tank columns invariably outran their supplies and exposed their flanks, a major worry of skeptics on the German General Staff, and a tank attack from the south by forces under Charles de Gaulle on May 18–19 and another from the north on May 21 by the British caused alarm. But tough German infantry repulsed these parries, enabling Guderian to reach the English Channel at Abbeville late on May 20.

The Germans now turned north along the coast. The Allies, still fighting but disorganized and without supplies, had to retreat to Dunkirk, where they received a gift when the Germans halted their attack for several days. This allowed Britain to send hundreds of vessels to evacuate its soldiers. By June 4 this "miracle of Dunkirk," protected by the Royal Air Force and the French First Army, had rescued 200,000 British troops and 140,000 others, mostly French.

The campaign for the Low Countries and Northern France took three weeks, about as long as the Polish campaign. The Wehrmacht now wheeled round for its final drive to complete the great circle that began in Austria: southward into the battered remnants of the French army.

## Legend

- German offensives
- Allied Forces movement
- Maginot Line
- Dutch canal area
- (44) Number of divisions

N

North Sea

ENGLAND

Zuider Zee

NETHERLANDS

Rotterdam

Meuse R.

ARMY GROUP B
(29)

GERMANY

Antwerp

Dunkirk

BELGIAN ARMY

Calais

FRENCH 7TH ARMY

Brussels

Boulogne

B.E.F. 21 MAY

BELGIUM

Fort Eben Emael

Rundstedt
ARMY GROUP A
(44)

FRENCH 1ST ARMY

Sambre R.

Rommel

Ardennes Forest

Cambrai

Dinant

Guderian

Abbeville

Sommes R.

FRENCH 9TH ARMY

Sedan

LUXEMBOURG

ARMY GROUP C
(17)

DE GAULLE
COUNTERATTACK, 18 MAY

FRENCH 2ND ARMY

Meuse R.

FRANCE

0        50 Miles

0        50 Kilometers

# 9 THE PARTITION OF FRANCE

On June 5, 1940, the Germans sent minor forces against the rear of the Maginot Line and then headed south, sweeping aside makeshift French defenses and prompting the flight of millions of civilians desperate to escape a repeat of the carnage of World War One. The French government declared Paris an "open city," meaning it would not be defended and so need not be destroyed, and resigned on June 16. Marshal Philippe Pétain, an aging hero of the Great War, became "head of state." On June 20 he signed an armistice limiting the French army to 100,000 men and committing France to pay all occupation costs.

The armistice divided France into three main parts. Germany occupied a zone containing the industrial north, the entire Atlantic coast, and the urbanized region around Paris. Italy, which opportunistically declared war on June 10, received the southeast plus Corsica. Except for detached slices in the north, the rest became "Unoccupied France," with a capital at Vichy and control of the police, the colonies, and the navy, which had capital ships in the Mediterranean. Vichy's quasi-fascist character—its Spain-like Catholic conservatism and its willingness to round up Jews and Communists for the Gestapo—would make it a target for bitter reprisals after the war. Charles de Gaulle, recently promoted to general, flew at the last minute to England to announce the forming of a "Free French" government in exile. Vichy court-martialed de Gaulle in absentia for treason and condemned him to death.

France became what historian John Keegan calls the "golden goose" of the Third Reich, which took half of all war-related French industrial production; most of its ships, aircraft, aluminum, motor vehicles, and rubber products; half of its steel and wood; and a large part of its woolens, chemicals, and hay. French iron ore made it less urgent for the Germans to buy Swedish ore; French gasoline let the Wehrmacht refuel until it could commandeer the oilfields of Rumania and Russia. French food—vegetable oils, wine, fish, meat, corn—fed the Reich for four years. French production equaled a quarter of the German gross national product. The cost was more than economic: Some 600,000 French died in the war, a third in combat; Vichy sent thousands to work in Germany, drafted thousands more for French mines and factories, and sent 75,000 Jews to concentration camps. By 1944 millions of French, amidst rich farmland, were malnourished.

How had this happened when France had strong fortifications, a larger army than Germany, as many tanks and planes as Germany, plus British help? The reasons are many, starting with the lack of both joint planning with Belgium and military coordination with Britain. But five other reasons stand out. First, unlike the Allies, the Germans concentrated their tanks and trucks in specialized divisions and then concentrated the divisions in a single sector. Once through the Ardennes, they traversed a region with good roads where distances were short and supply columns could keep up. Second, unlike the Allies, the Germans employed combined arms tactics: tanks, artillery, infantry, and especially planes. Stukas bombed roads and spread havoc, and Messerschmitt 109s strafed and pursued, both operating in close support of the ground forces. Third, French intelligence failed. France never learned that the Germans would drive through the Ardennes; they therefore had their weakest army in this "hinge" position for the panzers to shatter. Fourth, French communications and transportation were weak. Germany supplied its key units, including air squadrons, with radios for tactical coordination; France did not. Nor could French troops, lacking motor vehicles, move quickly to shore up crumbling sectors. Fifth, German soldiers, filled with vengeful and expansionist Nazi zeal and trained to seize the initiative, fought harder. Allied morale was good but not ferocious. France was willing but not eager to fight, and at point after point (as in the crossing of the Meuse in mid-May), that made a difference.

The fall of France was one of the great catastrophes of modern history. It made possible, in the words of historians Williamson Murray and Allan Millett, the "invasion of Russia and the Final Solution" and the near destruction of Western civilization.

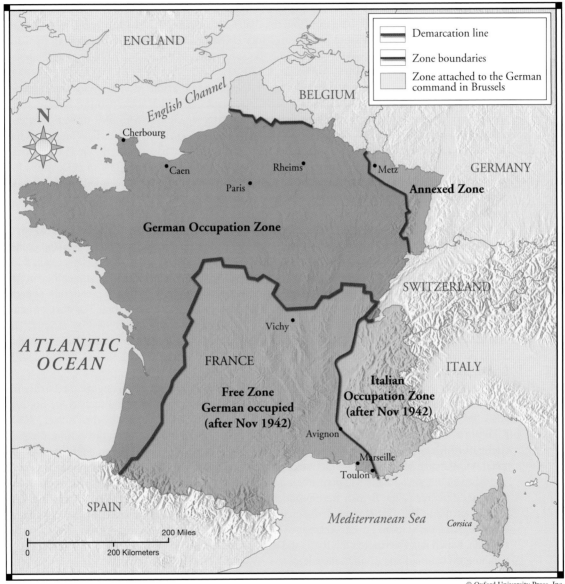

ENGLAND

BELGIUM

GERMANY

English Channel

N

Cherbourg

Caen

Rheims

Metz

Paris

**Annexed Zone**

**German Occupation Zone**

SWITZERLAND

ATLANTIC
OCEAN

Vichy

FRANCE

ITALY

**Free Zone
German occupied
(after Nov 1942)**

**Italian
Occupation Zone
(after Nov 1942)**

Avignon

SPAIN

Marseille

Toulon

Mediterranean Sea

Corsica

| | Demarcation line |
| | Zone boundaries |
| | Zone attached to the German command in Brussels |

0          200 Miles

0          200 Kilometers

© Oxford University Press, Inc.

# 10 THE BATTLE OF BRITAIN

Germany and Britain remained at war after June 1940. Crushing the British meant dealing with the English Channel, an obstacle to invaders for a millennium and the main reason Britain felt no urgency in forging an alliance with France until it was too late. But Britain's survival could lead to two developments that Germany dreaded: a two-front war, particularly if the United States came in, and a repeat of the naval blockade that nearly strangled Germany in World War One. If Hitler intended to invade, moreover, better in 1940 than later because the British army had left most of its equipment on the beaches at Dunkirk. In early July Hitler ordered his staff to develop an invasion plan for the fall. Its first task would be to secure the approaches to the island, including the Channel, which meant destroying the Royal Air Force (RAF).

Thus began the dramatic aerial conflict known by the name Prime Minister Winston Churchill gave it, the Battle of Britain. The Luftwaffe had 2,800 planes, of which some two-thirds were available at any one time. Nearly half were the excellent Messerschmitt (Me) 109 fighters, the rest mostly twin-engine bombers. (The Stuka dive bomber that was so effective in earlier campaigns had neither the range nor the speed for Channel fighting.) The fighter bases were on the French coast, the bombers farther back to avoid British counterattack and to allow the 109s to clear the skies. Britain had perhaps 700 fighter planes. Most were Hurricanes, a rugged plane good enough to take on the bombers; the rest were Spitfires, a nimble match for the 109s but in short supply (although English factories produced more over the course of the battle).

The conflict had several phases. During July and August, the Germans engaged the RAF over the Channel in an effort to weaken it by sheer attrition. But the Luftwaffe lost twice as many planes as the British and so began instead to target radar installations and then airfields. This evened the loss ratio to four to three but still failed to clear the skies. The Germans now took aim at the aircraft factories themselves, a tactic that produced some successes, as when a dozen plants in Coventry were destroyed in November. But the loss ratio climbed back to nearly two to one. For the Germans, it was a small next step from bombing factories to bombing cities in order to destroy morale. The "Blitz," which lasted until Hitler transferred his squadrons to the east in spring 1941, dropped 35,000 tons of explosives and millions of incendiaries (half of them on London), killed 45,000 British citizens, and caused much dislocation. Morale held.

The Germans failed partly because the 109s had limited range and could engage the enemy for only a few minutes even from forward French bases, not enough to kill a plane such as the Spitfire. Also, the engagements turned heavily on pilot skill, a more precious commodity than planes. When RAF pilots went down, the Royal Navy or local citizens rescued them for future action; downed Germans drowned or became prisoners of war (POWs). The two-engine German bombers also had small bomb loads, which doomed the factory and urban attacks to almost certain failure.

Above all, the Germans had poor intelligence. They overestimated how many planes they shot down and how many the British were producing, which was enough to keep RAF strength at 600 despite attrition. The Germans underestimated how the radar stations warned of attacks and so failed to make the stations sustained targets. They underestimated the impact of their attacks on the airfields, which nearly crippled the RAF, and they overestimated (like everyone else) the impact of bombing on national and civilian morale.

The conflict showed that Churchill's Britain would fight on despite pounding and privation. The Battle of Britain quelled all talk of accommodating Hitler. Equally important, it increased the sympathy of the Americans as well as the Dominions for their beleaguered, heroic "cousins," a sympathy on which Churchill increasingly counted for the salvation of his country.

# 11 THE BATTLE OF THE ATLANTIC

B ritain was an island, making it difficult to invade, but it needed maritime commerce for its prosperity and survival. Much of this commerce was with the British Empire, especially Asia, but also with the Western Hemisphere and Africa. The trade routes ran across the mid-Atlantic, down the African coast, past Gibraltar, and through the Suez Canal. The U.S. Lend-Lease Program made the Atlantic all the more vital; since much U.S. equipment was transshipped to the U.S.S.R., the Arctic route was vital as well. Britain nearly strangled Germany with a blockade 20 years earlier during the Great War. The Germans now tried to repay the favor by sinking enough merchant ships to strangle Britain. For a while they almost succeeded.

The first year and a half of the war was a "happy time" for the Kriegsmarine, which deployed surface raiders, mines, and submarines (U-boats) to sink nearly 250,000 tons of shipping per month. This was twice what Britain, then concentrating on aircraft, managed to add to the merchant fleet, a situation that the Royal Navy, its country reeling, sought urgently to change. The admiralty deployed minesweepers, sank German surface ships (including the giant battleship *Bismarck* in mid-1941), and established an air base in Iceland from which seaplanes could attack the U-boats when they surfaced. The British also organized the merchant vessels into 50-ship convoys with armed naval escorts. Merchant sinkings fell for several months.

But there were not enough escorts or planes (the RAF monopolized aircraft), and too much of the Atlantic lay beyond air reach. The Germans began to rely more on submarines, not surface ships, increasing their number and using "wolf pack" tactics. When a U-boat detected a convoy, it would radio the location. U-boats would then converge for an all-out attack, especially at night when it was hard to see submarines on the ocean's surface where the U-boats were faster and deadlier. German planes also hunted for convoys. U.S. entry into the war stepped up the flow of convoys, which offered additional tempting targets, including oil tankers sailing through the Caribbean from Texas and Venezuela without protective U.S. air patrols.

From early 1942 to mid-1943, the second "happy time" for U-boat crews, kills mushroomed to 500,000 tons a month. These came mainly north of Venezuela and off the eastern seaboard of the United States, where cities failed to "black out" at night, leaving the convoys sillouetted for German torpedoes. When U.S. cities enforced the blackout and the army released planes to hunt U-boats, the killings moved to the mid-Atlantic where the escorts remained sparse, a huge concern in late 1942 as the Allies transported troops and arms for the landings in North Africa.

But by early 1943 the United States was producing a million tons of new shipping per month (twice what the U-boats sank) and enough destroyers over and above Pacific needs to provide strong convoy escorts, including an occasional escort aircraft carrier. The United States also committed well-armed, long-range four-engine B24 bombers and squadrons of special PBY antisubmarine patrol planes for U-boat pursuit. The British added ships and planes of their own, and a base in the Azores, a Portuguese colony, closed the mid-Atlantic gap in air cover. Allied planes now carried radar that could detect U-boats that surfaced at night or in foul weather—precisely when the Germans liked to strike—and British code breakers were reading enough of the coded German radio traffic to anticipate "wolf pack" attacks. Merchant losses fell to 50,000 tons per month for the last two years of the war, a mere nuisance given the vast river of war materials flowing to Britain for Russia, for the Italian campaign, and for the great buildup to the D-Day landings, whose eventual success cost the Reich, among other things, its submarine pens on the French coast.

Germany lost 700 U-boats and 26,000 crewmen in the Battle of the Atlantic. The Allies lost 15 million tons of merchant shipping, 175 warships, over 40,000 naval seamen, and 30,000 merchantmen. These were among the highest death rates for any wartime service.

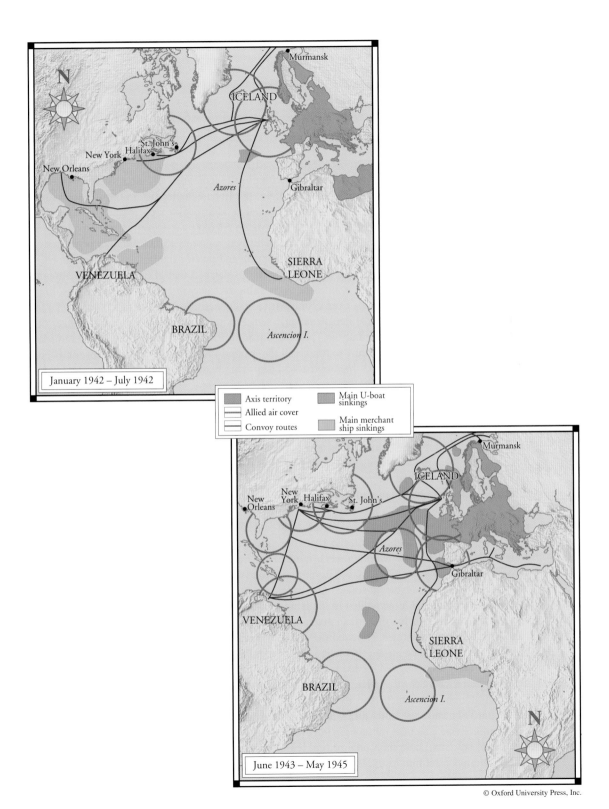

January 1942 – July 1942

| | |
|---|---|
| Axis territory | Main U-boat sinkings |
| Allied air cover | Main merchant ship sinkings |
| Convoy routes | |

June 1943 – May 1945

# 12 | THE DESERT WAR

The North African desert war highlighted another British vulnerability: its reliance on Egypt and the Suez Canal to reach its Asian interests, including food and raw materials from south and southeast Asia and oil from Persia (Iran) and Arabia. Threatening Suez meant threatening Britain's ability to hold its own and keep fighting. But the desert war exposed major weaknesses in the Italian part of the Axis equation and also in blitzkrieg warfare itself, which proved inadequate over the long empty spaces of Libya.

The struggle began in September 1940 with an attack from Libya into Egypt by the Italian army, a large but ill-trained and immobile force with obsolescent tanks and aircraft. The British had fewer troops and offered only modest resistance, but the Italians halted after 60 miles to resupply and never resumed their advance. Britain scraped together additional troops, including some armor, for a "5-day raid" that turned into a major offensive. In 61 days the Desert Army advanced 500 miles along the coastal roads of the great hump of Libya, captured 130,000 Italian prisoners and mountains of supplies, occupied the key port of Tobruk, and pushed the Italians past Benghazi.

Two events conspired to reverse things. Churchill—alarmed that Hitler had drawn Hungary, Rumania, Bulgaria, and Yugoslavia into the Axis orbit and was preparing to help Mussolini in Greece and Crete—ordered troops from North Africa to Greece, a move that failed to hold Greece but weakened the Desert Army. Hitler meanwhile sent Erwin Rommel with two crack panzer divisions and air support to bolster Italy in Libya. Ever bold, Rommel immediately counterattacked, using vigorous flanking movements to retake all the ground just lost and more, except for Tobruk, which grimly held. In April 1941, having reached Egypt but with his fuel running low and defenses stiffening, Rommel halted.

Britain took the field again in late 1941 with a new commander, an infusion of Lend-Lease equipment, and fresh divisions. Rommel retreated to a point west of Benghazi, but the Desert Army, weakened by its own supply problems and the diversion of forces to the Far East to face Japan, could not follow through. Rommel was now avid to seize Suez, and he was confident that he could outmaneuver the British on the southern end of their defensive positions and stop their counterattacks by using the vaunted 88-mm antiaircraft gun as an antitank weapon. He therefore went on the offensive, grinding out a major advance and finally taking Tobruk.

The British stopped the bleeding only after fierce fighting at El Alamein, mere miles from Alexandria. The stage was thus set for the sixth and final push in this strange seesaw war. This began on October 23, 1942, when the British 8th Army, newly christened and under yet another commander (Bernard Law Montgomery), jumped off for an offensive that would ultimately clear Libya of Axis troops.

The Desert War revealed some hard truths about armored warfare. Because the vehicles consumed fuel that had to be hauled to the front, blitzkrieg worked best over short distances, as in Poland or France. Over North African distances, the system did not work; the result was a "rubber band" effect whereby armies stretched their supply lines to the breaking point and then "snapped back" to their original position. Also, blitzkrieg worked in Europe partly by sowing mass confusion among civilians, who clogged the roads and prevented mobilization and movement. In a thinly populated region such as North Africa, this did not happen, leaving enemy communications and transportation strained but intact. And the Germans enjoyed air superiority in Europe but not in the desert, partly because the Luftwaffe was busy attacking the island of Malta.

Rommel was a tactical but not a strategic or logistical genius. He did not have the strength or supplies to seize and hold the Canal or link with German forces in Russia, and most General Staff officers did not want him to try. In making the attempt, he exposed the entire Axis position on the African continent.

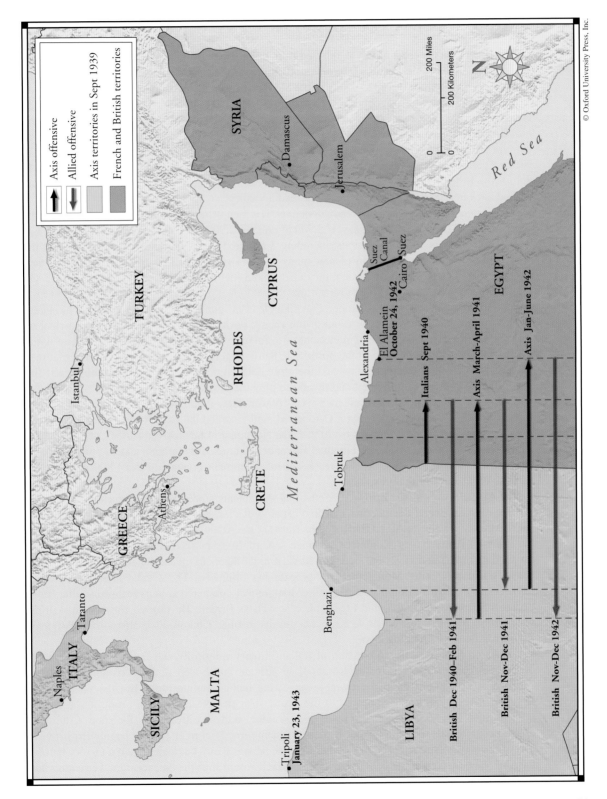

# 13 THE BATTLE OF EL ALAMEIN

El Alamein, on the coast of Egypt, differed from other positions in the desert campaigns because the vast impassable Qattara Depression 40 miles to the south precluded the wide flanking movements that Rommel loved as surely as the Mediterreanean did in the north. With so constricted a front, the battle became a "set piece" in which preparation and firepower rather than surprise and bold movement would shape the outcome. This suited the talents of Bernard Law Montgomery, the new British commander, a methodical man determined (despite Churchill's badgering) not to move until he had rebuilt the morale and resources of his army. Monty had little interest in daring tactics because daring could produce defeat as well as victory. Africa was a minor theater for Hitler, but not for the British. Driven out of Europe, battered by air and sea, overwhelmed in East Asia, and pushed back in Africa, Britain desperately needed a victory.

By October Montgomery was ready to deliver. His men were well trained, and he had material superiority: 1,000 tanks, including new U.S. M4 Shermans; 2,000 field and antitank guns; 500 planes; and 200,000 men in 10-plus divisions, including 3 armored divisions. The Axis, though equal in guns, had only half the tanks and planes, many of them outmoded Italian models, and half the infantry, three-quarters of them Italian; they also lacked fuel. Rommel tried to compensate for all this by seeding his defense with a million mines.

Montgomery opened up on October 23 with a thousand-gun night barrage against the Axis left about 8 miles inland, the strongest point of the enemy position. Infantry was to follow to clear a path for the armor. A vigorous feint in the south was intended to hold Axis forces in that sector until the British tanks broke through in the north. The battle largely conformed to plan except that the minefields slowed the British infantry and therefore delayed the armor, allowing Rommel to redirect the German tanks from his right northward to plug the growing gap. The British responded by turning north toward the sea to draw away Axis power. They then returned to the original line of assault, breached the Axis defenses on October 30, and enlarged the gap on November 2. By now Rommel was outnumbered in tanks by 20 to 1. On November 4 he received Hitler's permission to withdraw. Montgomery, his troops bloodied and in heavy rains, did not immediately pursue, which allowed elements of the Axis forces to reach Tunisia. Rommel's conduct of this 1,800-mile retreat was one of his most brilliant exploits.

El Alamein shows two British strengths that the defeats since 1940 had obscured. One was "ULTRA," a top-secret deciphering machine capable of cracking coded German radio transmissions. Already of value to Allied leaders in the Battle of the Atlantic, ULTRA proved itself in Africa, too. The 8th Army halted Rommel's advance toward Suez partly because ULTRA intercepts revealed its timing and direction, signaling Royal Navy officers to increase their attacks on enemy convoys and prompting Montgomery to prepare his offensive. The second strength was the resources of the British Empire. At Alamein, Montgomery commanded units from Australia, New Zealand, South Africa, India, and Free France as well as Britain. He showed formidable skill in welding this jumble into a cohesive army. The results justified Churchill's contention in 1940 that Britain would not be fighting alone.

Alamein reinforced the impression of Italian military inferiority and fed the open contempt of German commanders, including Rommel, an attitude that boded ill for Axis solidarity. The Americans, by contrast, helped provide some of the battle-winning tools. But the victory was Britain's, and though small compared to the titanic struggles on the Eastern Front, it was much needed. Suez was secure, morale rejuvenated, Rommel bested, Libya taken for good. Churchill ordered church bells rung throughout Britain. Alamein turned out to be the last largely British victory of the war. Monty attacked in October because he was ready but also to gain a victory before the Americans arrived in the field in November, which would shift the balance of power within the English-speaking alliance for all time.

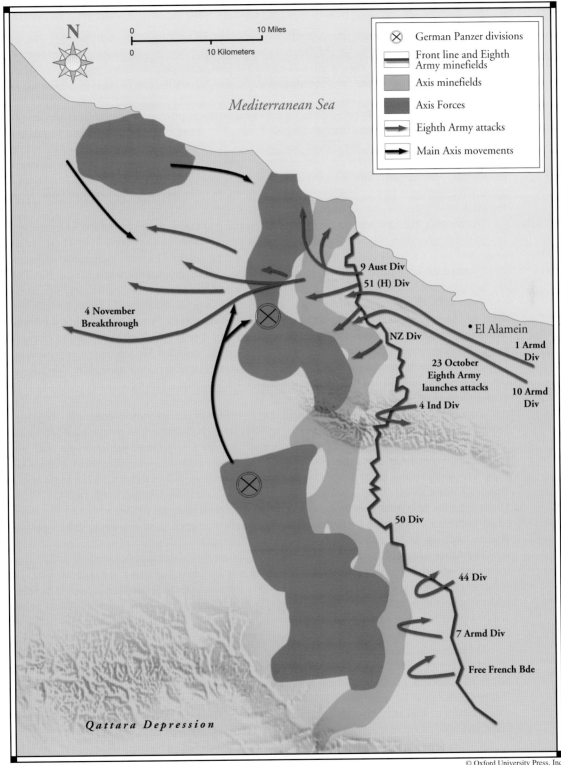

German Panzer divisions

Front line and Eighth
Army minefields

Axis minefields

Axis Forces

Eighth Army attacks

Main Axis movements

N

0        10 Miles

0        10 Kilometers

*Mediterranean Sea*

9 Aust Div

51 (H) Div

• El Alamein

NZ Div

1 Armd
Div

4 November
Breakthrough

23 October
Eighth Army
launches attacks

10 Armd
Div

4 Ind Div

50 Div

44 Div

7 Armd Div

Free French Bde

*Qattara Depression*

© Oxford University Press, Inc.

# 14 THE CONQUEST OF NORTH AFRICA

Safe behind the oceans and preoccupied in the 1920s with making money and in the 1930s with dealing with the ravages of the Depression, the United States only haltingly overcame the impulses that kept it from joining the League of Nations, enlarging its army, supporting Loyalist Spain, or permitting weapons sales to Britain and France. It took the fall of Poland and France and the prospect of Nazi domination in Europe to change America's outlook.

But change it did. Congress enacted a naval rearmament program and extended-service conscription in 1940 and the massive Lend-Lease Program in March 1941, and President Franklin D. Roosevelt arranged a deal to furnish destroyers to Britain. The administration began a crash construction program to make the United States, in Franklin Roosevelt's phrase, "the arsenal of democracy." In August 1941 Roosevelt enunciated a policy of "Four Freedoms"—freedom of speech, freedom of religion, freedom from want, freedom from fear—that placed the United States unmistakably in the anti-Nazi camp.

Roosevelt's main interest was in halting the Nazis. War came, however, not from Germany but from Germany's Asian ally, Japan, which attacked Pearl Harbor on December 7, 1941. Hitler and Mussolini soon declared war on the United States, and an Anglo-American conference in January 1942 agreed on a "Europe first" strategy that would include combat in North Africa. But Pearl Harbor and other Japanese victories in early 1942 alarmed Washington, and public pressure built to focus on the Pacific. Making matters worse, some American generals opposed a North African operation on the grounds that it would delay an invasion of northwest France and commit the United States to a wasteful peripheral strategy. Moreover, no one knew what Vichy's troops, in charge of France's North African colonies, would do. But Churchill wanted a Mediterranean approach, and FDR wanted Americans to fight the Germans somewhere in 1942 to relieve a bleeding U.S.S.R. and before public opinion forced him mostly toward the Pacific. Since Europe was out of the question, Africa would have to do.

The landings, under General Dwight D. Eisenhower as overall commander, began on November 8 with the goal of taking Tunisia, an Axis stronghold. American troops went ashore in a sector of French Morocco around Casablanca and in Algeria near Oran; British troops and more Americans targeted Algiers farther east. Despite diplomatic efforts to neutralize them, many Vichy French resisted, killing 1,500 Americans and scuttling the French fleet rather than turning it over to Britain. Efforts to establish a provisional French administration faltered until the Free French leader, Charles de Gaulle, was brought in. The United States objected to this, a blunder that would cause problems with France for half a century. Germany occupied all of France, to deflect possible Riviera landings, and reinforced Tunisia.

The Allies advanced rapidly, nearing Tunis in January 1943. But supplies ran low, and German troops joined with Rommel's army from Libya to thrash the green Americans at Kasserine Pass. The setback was temporary. Montgomery overwhelmed Rommel near eastern Tunisia, and U.S. forces under a new tank-oriented commander, George S. Patton, drove hard from the west. Allied air and sea power all but stopped Axis supply convoys. The Axis surrendered in Africa in May 1943; the Allies took 250,000 prisoners at a cost of 75,000 casualties.

The campaign underscored the value both of Malta, whose survival provided a base for British air and sea power, and of ULTRA, which helped Montgomery best Rommel and helped British planes and ships attack Axis convoys with astonishing precision. Eisenhower proved a gifted Allied leader; Patton's prowess as an armored commander began to reveal itself. Rommel's reputation for chivalrous behavior as well as brilliant tactics endured, although this was partly a function of an empty landscape and little racial venom—fewer civilian victims meant less gratuitous brutality.

Winning also helped. El Alamein, together with Stalingrad, persuaded some Vichy commanders to throw in with the Allies. Franco, ever the opportunist, refused to let Germans cross Spain to attack Gibraltar, guaranteeing safe Allied passage through the Straits. What Churchill called the "Tunisgrad" surrender was the result.

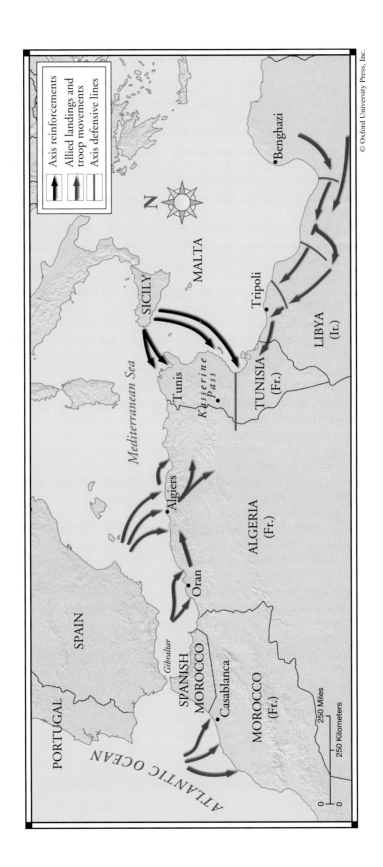

# 15 Barbarossa—The Invasion of the U.S.S.R.

Hitler's invasion of the Soviet Union expanded the war and made it more savage. His reasons for attacking were many. He hated Marxism as a divisive internationalist ideology antithetical to German nationalism and associated it in his own mind with the hated Jews—"Jewish Bolshevism." The Soviets were also mostly Slavs, "subhumans" (in Hitler's view) like the Poles, whose destiny was to labor for the "master race." Also Hitler had long preached the need for *lebensraum* (living space) for Germans. Russia was that space and would provide resources—grain, metals, and especially petroleum—that the Reich, despite controlling most of Europe, still needed for its war economy. Hitler proposed, in a word, to "Africanize" the Soviet Union: to subjugate, colonize, and exploit it. If he could prevent a two-front war, all the better.

But the U.S.S.R. was a vast semi-industrialized foe, able despite famines and purges to muster millions of men and vehicles. Hitler and Stalin had negotiated a nonaggression and trade agreement in 1939 that gave Stalin eastern Poland and gave Hitler Soviet raw materials while attacking the West. The pact meant little to Hitler. Stalin took it seriously enough to disregard warnings of a German attack and seems to have been briefly incapacitated by the shock of the onslaught.

On June 22 3 million Germans crossed into the U.S.S.R. Army Group North, with the 4th Panzer Army, moved from East Prussia north through the Baltic states toward Leningrad (St. Petersburg). Army Group South, with the 1st Panzer Army, moved from Czechoslovakia and Hungary southeast into the Ukraine, the Soviet breadbasket, and toward the Black Sea port of Sevastopol. The strongest force, Army Group Center with the 2nd and 3rd Panzer Armies, moved from Poland toward Minsk and Smolensk, and beyond that, toward Moscow. Facing them were 4 million Red Army troops as well as thousands of guns, tanks, and planes, most of which were obsolescent but were there nonetheless.

Conceived in the blitzkrieg spirit, the invasion confronted two obstacles: distances and the Red Army. The distances spoke for themselves. Although the attack would unfold over ideal armored terrain, if sustained to the end, it would create 700-mile supply lines (longer than even those of North Africa) and a 900-mile front too extended for even the Wehrmacht to man. The Red Army, too, was immense. But it was in disarray because Stalin had purged the officer corps and scattered the armor among the infantry in World War One fashion. It was also packed close to the frontier, making defense in depth difficult. In the end Hitler decreed not an all-out thrust into the far interior, as in pure blitzkrieg, but a pincer-and-envelopment strategy to trap and annihilate the Red Army where it stood. If that could be accomplished, the cities and industrial areas would fall in a few months.

The strategy nearly worked. In the north the Germans inflicted 400,000 casualties and invested Leningrad with orders to level every building and starve the population. At the center, the panzers encircled Minsk in late June and Smolensk by the end of July, killing or capturing a million Russians and destroying thousands of vehicles, tanks, and guns. The southern advance ground forward more slowly against stronger defenses, so Hitler, in a controversial move, diverted armies, including the 2nd Panzer Army, from the center to help trap defenders around Kiev and speed the approach to the Black Sea. The yield was 1.5 million Soviet casualties.

But appearances were misleading. Hundreds of thousands of Soviet soldiers escaped the encirclements and kept fighting. Leningrad and Sevastopol held. Moscow raised new divisions and orchestrated an astonishing relocation of factories by rail to safer regions beyond the Volga River. The Wehrmacht suffered 400,000 casualties, ammunition and fuel ran short, and the tanks broke down at an alarming rate. It was under these circumstances that Hitler concentrated his forces, including three of the four panzer armies, for a final drive on Moscow.

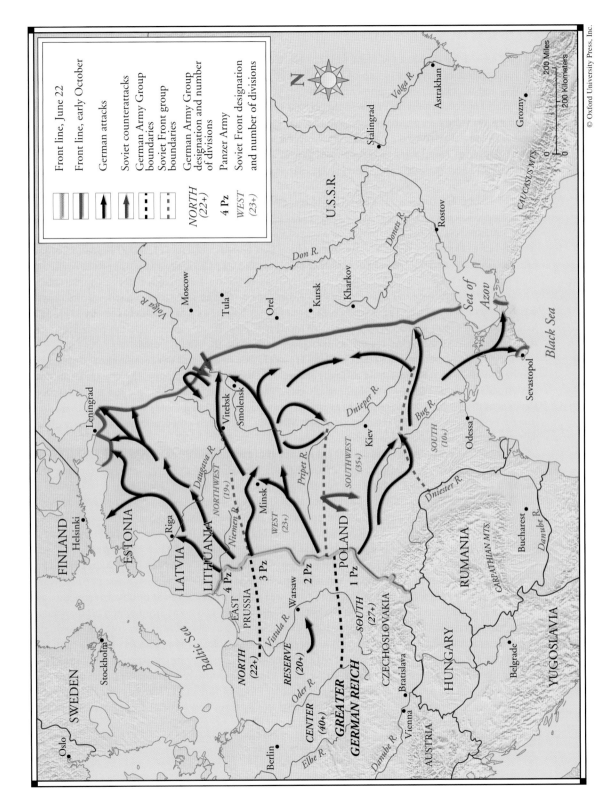

Front line, June 22

Front line, early October

German attacks

Soviet counterattacks

German Army Group boundaries

Soviet Front group boundaries

*NORTH* (22+) German Army Group designation and number of divisions

**4 Pz** Panzer Army

*WEST* (23+) Soviet Front designation and number of divisions

N

SWEDEN

Oslo

Stockholm

FINLAND

Helsinki

Baltic Sea

ESTONIA

LATVIA

Riga

LITHUANIA

Leningrad

*Daugava R.*

*NORTHWEST* (19+)

*Niemen R.*

EAST PRUSSIA

4 Pz

3 Pz

Warsaw

*Vistula R.*

2 Pz

Minsk

*WEST* (23+)

Vitebsk

Smolensk

*Pripet R.*

*Dnieper R.*

*Volga R.*

Moscow

Tula

Orel

Kursk

Kharkov

*Don R.*

*Donets R.*

U.S.S.R.

Stalingrad

*Volga R.*

Astrakhan

Grozny

*CAUCASUS MTS.*

Rostov

Sea of Azov

Sevastopol

Black Sea

*SOUTHWEST* (35+)

Kiev

*Bug R.*

*SOUTH* (10+)

Odessa

*Dniester R.*

1 Pz

POLAND

*SOUTH* (27+)

NORTH (22+)

RESERVE (20+)

CENTER (40+)

*Oder R.*

GREATER GERMAN REICH

Berlin

*Elbe R.*

CZECHOSLOVAKIA

Bratislava

Vienna

AUSTRIA

*Danube R.*

HUNGARY

RUMANIA

*CARPATHIAN MTS.*

Bucharest

*Danube R.*

Belgrade

YUGOSLAVIA

200 Miles

0

200 Kilometers

0

# 16 THE DRIVE ON MOSCOW

The Axis drive on Moscow went well at first. German armor pushed past the heavily defended rail centers of Bryansk (south of Moscow) and Vyazma (just west), captured another 650,000 POWs, and wrecked more equipment. But by late October it was raining, which turned the primitive roads into quagmires and slowed the assault until a winter freeze hardened the surfaces. Axis columns, now moving again, created salients (protrusions in the line) just north of the capital and around the lower edge of the city of Tula 75 miles to the south. Forward units could see the spires of the Kremlin. The Soviet government began to evacuate its offices. But Tula held, and so did Moscow. In late November, the winter deepened and froze engine oil, fuel lines, and firing mechanisms. The Wehrmacht, bone-weary, sick, and cold, ground to a halt.

On December 6, General Georgi Zhukov, commander-in-chief of the Soviet western front (including Moscow's defenses), launched a startling counterattack with reorganized Russian air force squadrons, significant numbers of an outstanding new Russian tank (the T34), and infantry from Siberia. German Army Group Center, which had already sustained 150,000 casualties since October, buckled and fell back. Other counterattacks pushed the Germans away from Rostov, on the Don River above the Sea of Azov, and won breathing space for Leningrad. But the counterattack was too ambitious given the massive losses of men, materiel, and industrial capacity of the previous six months. By spring the Soviets, too, ground to a halt, impeded like their foes by rain, and lack of supplies, and in the Soviets' case, by too few trucks. Efforts to encircle the panzer armies and retake cities such as Orel (in the center) and Kharkov (to the south) failed.

Nevertheless, Germany lost the Battle of Moscow. One reason was the combination of distance and bad roads, which made supply difficult and vehicle breakdowns a plague, thereby undermining the effectiveness of blitzkrieg's slashing attacks. The widening front, too, played a role. When Hitler sent troops southward against Kiev in late summer, it took the infantry weeks to get there and more weeks to get back into position to attack Moscow. The much-noted weather—rain as well as subzero temperatures—made everything worse.

None of this would have mattered except for the unanticipated resistance of the Red Army, which took enormous casualties but inflicted them too, slowing the invasion and sapping the strength of the Wehrmacht, which had never faced this kind of fighting. And there was Zhukov, a coarse, domineering, aggressive commander who imposed martial law on Moscow, sent tens of thousands of women into the cold to dig antitank ditches, and persuaded Stalin to counterattack. Zhukov would become the U.S.S.R.'s most famous soldier, one of the few men who could contest Stalin and survive, the most successful general in the most important theater of the war.

The map shows another factor in the German defeat: the "guerrillas," or partisans, who attacked supply columns and outposts and blew up railroads behind the German lines. Partisan warfare, a striking feature of the entire Eastern Front, was partly a natural result of blitzkrieg tactics, in which the mechanized columns left in their wake large unsubdued areas from which civilians and Red Army remnants could mount hit-and-run ambushes. It was also a response to Nazi ideology. The Germans were brutal conquerers, not liberators. Hitler told his commanders to kill "anyone who looks askance at a German," especially Communists. *Einsatzgruppen* (special SS units) systematically murdered Jews, often with army help. Germans destroyed villages, ransacked towns, stole at will, and perpetrated mass hangings. Of the millions of Soviet POWs, only one in three survived. The partisans fought, even in anti-Stalinist areas, from fear, patriotism, and zeal and for revenge—and because they had nothing to lose.

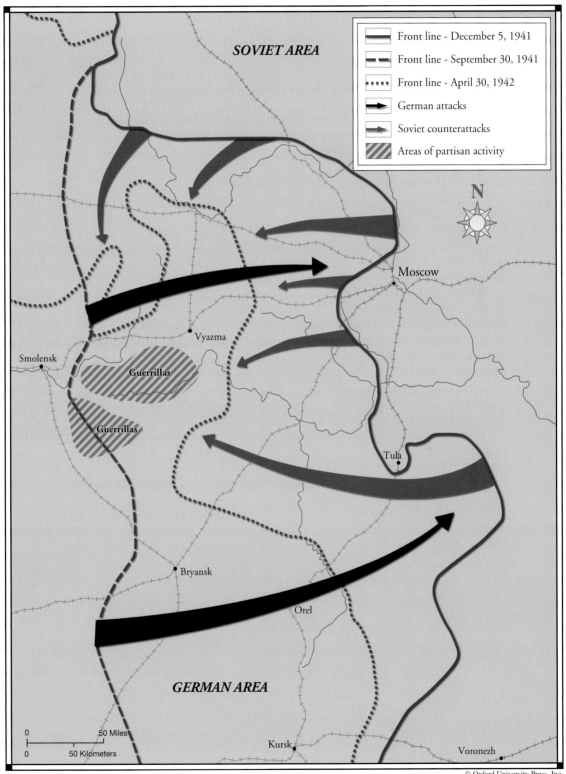

Front line - December 5, 1941

Front line - September 30, 1941

Front line - April 30, 1942

German attacks

Soviet counterattacks

Areas of partisan activity

N

Moscow

Vyazma

Smolensk

Guerrillas

Guerrillas

Tula

Bryansk

Orel

GERMAN AREA

0        50 Miles

0        50 Kilometers

Kursk

Voronezh

# 17 THE CAUCASUS CAMPAIGN

J ust as Hitler shifted in 1941 from destroying the Red Army to seizing Moscow, he shifted in 1942 from seizing Moscow to conquering the southern U.S.S.R., including the Caucasus, the source of nearly all the Soviet Union's petroleum. This was predictable given the paucity of European oil reserves. The mechanization of all national armies produced an insatiable thirst for oil, the life blood of internal combustion engines and therefore of armored, motorized formations and all naval and air fleets. Initially a means to strategic ends, oil became a strategic end in itself, a chief reason for Britain's defense of Suez and the convoys, of Japan's invasion of South East Asia, of America's bombing of Reich refineries, of Germany's control of Rumania—and of the German lunge in 1942 for the oil wells of the Caucasus. A secondary objective was Stalingrad, a manufacturing city astride the Volga River, the main oil transport artery for the Russian heartland.

As usual, the summer campaigning went well for the Germans, who pushed a large Soviet force back to Voronezh, took 240,000 prisoners east of Kharkov, and captured another 170,000 in front of Sevastopol, which capitulated in early July. The 4$^{th}$ and 1$^{st}$ Panzer Armies now drove almost unopposed down the featureless grassy steppe between the Donets and the Don, taking the oil center of Maikop in early August and reaching the Caspian wells around Grozny two weeks later. Visions of Astrakhan and a breakthrough to the Persian oil fields danced in Hitler's eyes.

This period saw the maximum German territorial conquests in the U.S.S.R., a near repeat of Imperial Germany's gains in World War One, and the high tide (with the advances in Africa and Asia) of Axis global domination. It also marked a new low in Soviet economic fortunes. The German drives into the Ukraine and Caucasus did substantial industrial damage and reduced oil supplies. They also curtailed Soviet food production. Relocated factories were producing enough weapons to outfit the Red Army, though not much else. But by the end of 1942, the average Russian was consuming only a thousand calories a day, well below minimum life requirements. American Lend-Lease food was beginning to trickle in, but unless something changed, the Soviet Union was on the verge of starving to death.

Problems were mounting for the Germans, too. The Soviets wrecked the Maikop wells, from which not a drop ever reached the Reich. By mid-July the panzers were winning few battles because they fought few—the Red Army was withdrawing to conserve its strength, leaving the Germans to conquer, as a Wehrmacht officer said, "mere empty land." Supply lines, on the other hand, were long, making even Luftwaffe deliveries difficult. Then on July 28 Stalin issued Order No. 227 demanding "No More Retreat," a harsh directive that suffused the Red Army with a bitter combativeness that showed itself in the mountain passes of the Caucasus and at Stalingrad. However, Stalingrad itself was becoming a problem, as the Reich would soon discover.

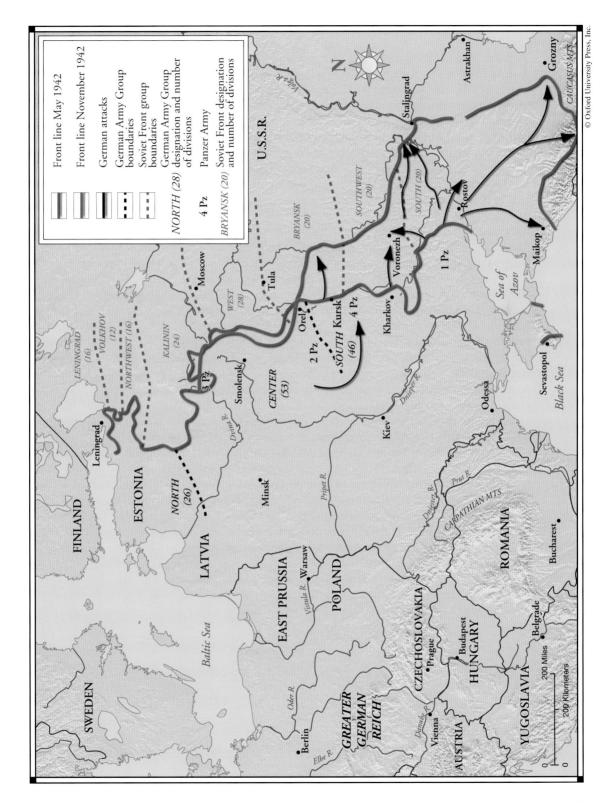

Legend:

Front line May 1942
Front line November 1942
German attacks
German Army Group boundaries
Soviet Front group boundaries
*NORTH* (28) German Army Group designation and number of divisions
**4 Pz** Panzer Army
*BRYANSK* (20) Soviet Front designation and number of divisions

N

U.S.S.R.

FINLAND

SWEDEN

Leningrad

*LENINGRAD (16)*
*VOLKHOV (12)*
*NORTHWEST (16)*
*KALININ (24)*
*WEST (28)*

ESTONIA

LATVIA

*NORTH (26)*

Moscow

Tula

3 Pz

Smolensk

*BRYANSK (20)*

Orel

2 Pz

*CENTER (53)*

*SOUTH (46)*

Kursk

4 Pz

*SOUTHWEST (20)*

Voronezh

*SOUTH (20)*

Stalingrad

Astrakhan

Grozny

*CAUCASUS MTS.*

Rostov

Maikop

1 Pz

Kharkov

Kiev

Sea of Azov

Dnieper R.

Minsk

Pripet R.

EAST PRUSSIA

POLAND

Warsaw

Vistula R.

Odessa

Sevastopol

Black Sea

Dniester R.

Prut R.

CARPATHIAN MTS.

ROMANIA

Bucharest

CZECHOSLOVAKIA

Prague

HUNGARY

Budapest

Belgrade

YUGOSLAVIA

AUSTRIA

Vienna

Danube R.

GREATER GERMAN REICH

Berlin

Elbe R.

Oder R.

Baltic Sea

Dvina R.

Volga R.

0       200 Miles
0       200 Kilometers

39

# 18 | The Stalingrad Campaign

Hitler assigned Stalingrad to the 20 divisions of the 6th Army, which would move eastward from the Donets with flanking support on its right from the 4th Panzer, the weakest of the German tank forces. By late September the Germans had reached the river and controlled much of the city, which the Luftwaffe had mostly pulverized except for three immense factories running along the west bank. Hitler did not normally permit his armies to fight street by street in cities because it neutralized their skills and speed. But this city bore Joseph Stalin's name and proved irresistible, so 6th Army labored on throughout October and early November despite losing half its combat strength in bitter fighting with the Soviet 62nd Army under General Vasily Chuikov.

Unknown to the Germans, the struggle was part of a plan concocted by Zhukov and the Soviet leaders to trap and annihilate 6th Army. Hitler no longer had enough troops in Russia to do everything he wanted; he therefore strengthened 6th Army by stripping German formations from the flanks and replacing them with Axis allies—in the south Rumanians, in the north Hungarians and Rumanians, with an Italian army in between (to keep them from fighting each other). The Soviets believed, rightly, that these were weak forces and stealthily built up powerful opposing armies on the east bank with orders to attack once 6th Army was too enmeshed to escape. At Stalingrad, meanwhile, just enough supplies and replacements came across the Volga each night to enable Chuikov's army, now fighting almost entirely from trenches, tunnels, factory floors, and cellars of smashed buildings, to hold on against 6th Army's still-formidable attacks.

The Soviet counteroffensive began November 19 with a 3,000-gun barrage. Both Rumanian armies instantly collapsed; the Hungarians and Italians soon followed. Four days later the pincers closed far to the west, leaving 6th Army surrounded. Its commander asked permission to break out. Hitler instead ordered forces under Erich von Manstein to break in while the Luftwaffe flew in supplies. Manstein, who had excelled in Poland, France, and Russia, drove his three tank divisions near enough to the ruined city to hear artillery. But in late December, with no sign that 6th Army was advancing to meet him, Manstein retreated under fierce ground and air attack.

Thus began the first of the German disasters on the Eastern Front. In the far south, the 1st Panzer Army withdrew from the Caspian back toward the Don to avoid being cut off. The 17th Army soon followed suit, abandoning the Maikop oil fields. At Stalingrad the Russians opened a 7,000-gun assault, the largest artillery barrage in history. On January 30 they overran the German headquarters; 100,000 German soldiers passed into Soviet hands, bringing the total loss (including Axis allies) to 300,000. The Luftwaffe lost 500 planes and 1,000 pilots. A German officer called Stalingrad the "graveyard of the Wehrmacht." In Germany, state radio played funereal music for three days.

In Moscow the bells of the Kremlin rang in celebration. Stalingrad was a real victory: It kept the Volga open, it weakened the Wehrmacht, and it showed that a nation willing to pay the price in planning and blood could win.

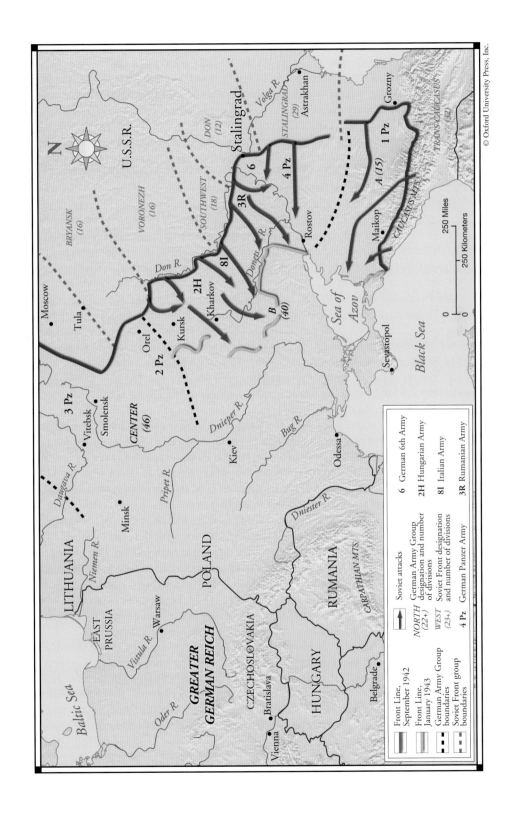

Baltic Sea

LITHUANIA

EAST
PRUSSIA

GREATER
GERMAN REICH

POLAND

CZECHOSLOVAKIA

HUNGARY

RUMANIA

Black Sea

Sea of
Azov

U.S.S.R.

N

Moscow

Tula

Orel

Kursk

Kharkov

Smolensk

Vitebsk

Minsk

Kiev

Odessa

Sevastopol

Belgrade

Bratislava

Vienna

Warsaw

Stalingrad

Astrakhan

Grozny

Maikop

Rostov

Don R.

Dnieper R.

Donets R.

Volga R.

Pripet R.

Bug R.

Dniester R.

Niemen R.

Daugava R.

Vistula R.

Oder R.

CARPATHIAN MTS.

CAUCASUS MTS.

TRANS-CAUCASUS
(32)

CENTER
(46)

BRYANSK
(16)

VORONEZH
(16)

SOUTHWEST
(18)

DON
(12)

STALINGRAD
(29)

3 Pz

2 Pz

2H

8I

3R

6

4 Pz

1 Pz

A (15)

B
(40)

250 Miles
250 Kilometers
0

| | |
|---|---|
| Front Line, September 1942 | |
| Front Line, January 1943 | |
| German Army Group boundaries | |
| Soviet Front group boundaries | |

Soviet attacks

NORTH
(22+)

German Army Group
designation and number
of divisions

WEST
(23+)

Soviet Front designation
and number of divisions

4 Pz German Panzer Army

6 German 6th Army

2H Hungarian Army

8I Italian Army

3R Rumanian Army

# 19 KURSK

After crushing the German 6th Army on the Volga, the Soviets drove toward the Donets River in the spring of 1943, threatening to retake Kharkov and push the Germans back to the Dnieper. But rain was falling, and as the Germans withdrew, their lines of communication shortened in the classic military manner while those of the Russians lengthened. The Red Army advance slowed, and Field Marshal Manstein, in command of the 1st and 4th Panzer Armies and a reconstituted 6th Army, succeeded in fixing the front with a brilliant "counterattack in retreat," one of the most challenging warfare maneuvers. Meanwhile, a costly Zhukov-engineered offensive against Army Group Center gained territory only around Kursk, a transportation hub halfway between Orel and Kharkov, both still under German occupation.

The result was a double salient, with a German bulge protruding east beyond Orel and a Soviet bulge punched west beyond Kursk. After toying briefly with the idea of attacking into the Orel salient, the Russians settled on action at Kursk. But arguments raged in each camp as to whether to attack or defend. At first, over the reservations of senior officers, Hitler and Stalin both urged attack. Stalin eventually acquiesced; Hitler did not. Germany would attack, thereby precipitating the largest armored battle in history.

The Germans proposed to hit the flanks of the salient with massive force and seal off and destroy the armies in the pocket, as had happened during the previous two summers, but things were not the same. The U.S.S.R. was producing 2,000 armored vehicles per month from its trans-Volga factories, so despite losses of 19,000 tanks, there were still 10,000 tanks in the field, two-fifths of them at Kursk. Most were the splendid T34s, with sloping armor to deflect shots, wide treads for traction in mud, a big 76- or 85-mm gun, and, most important, a 250-mile range that reduced the need to stop to refuel, a tank's most vulnerable moment. Although the Germans fielded 3,000 tanks (and 1,800 planes) at Kursk, they were producing far fewer per month than Russia.

Hitler hoped to compensate with the Panther, a fast up-gunned medium tank, and the huge Tiger, a slow but heavily armored tank mounting the vaunted 88 cannon. Hitler delayed the attack until July 5 in order to deploy more of these, but the Panthers broke down a lot and the lumbering Tigers proved vulnerable when the T34s converged at close range. Both were hard hit by rocket-firing Sturmovik aircraft, as good a "tank buster" as even the Luftwaffe could muster. The Soviets, moreover, constructed staggering defenses in depth—three lines of field fortifications with ditches and wire, 1 million mines, 13,000 fieldpieces and mortars, and powerful reserves to exploit German weaknesses. Zhukov also had good intelligence on the timing of the attack.

By July 7 panzers from the north had fought through to high ground above Kursk and from the south to within 50 miles of Kursk. But losses were enormous on both sides, the Russians were feeding in reserves, and the attack ground down. On July 13 Hitler transferred an elite unit to the defense of Italy and signaled the end of the operation. By July 23 the Germans were back where they had started, and the Russians were positioned to launch an offensive on a broad front, including against the Orel salient and toward Kharkov.

Some historians consider the Battle of Kursk the true turning point of the war: The Soviets lost 900,000 men and 6,000 tanks at Kursk and in the follow-up assaults, but they turned back a Nazi summer offensive for the first time, killed tens of thousands of German infantry and tankers and hundreds of scarce pilots, and did irreparable damage to the panzers. Reich factories would eventually replace the lost armor but not, after Kursk, add net strength. The Germans were still savage and resourceful foes, and much death awaited, but the results of Kursk meant that the heady days of Nazi conquest were over.

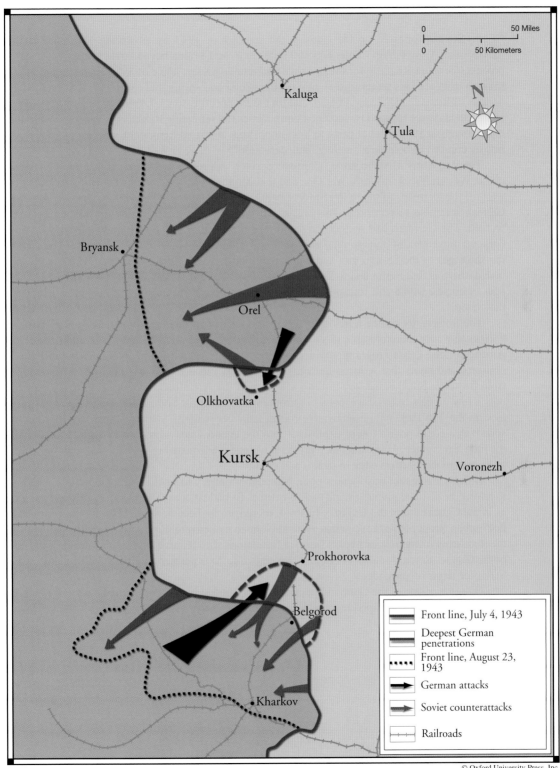

Kaluga

Tula

Bryansk

Orel

Olkhovatka

Kursk

Voronezh

Prokhorovka

Belgorod

Kharkov

N

0       50 Miles

0       50 Kilometers

| | |
|---|---|
| ▬ | Front line, July 4, 1943 |
| | Deepest German penetrations |
| ▪▪▪▪ | Front line, August 23, 1943 |
| ➤ | German attacks |
| ➤ | Soviet counterattacks |
| ┼┼┼ | Railroads |

# 20 The Soviets Move West

The Soviets followed up the gains in the summer of 1943 by advancing 150 miles against German Army Group Center and 300 miles into the Ukraine beyond the Dnieper River, in the process liberating Kharkov for the last time and retaking Kiev, scene of an overwhelming German triumph in 1941. This set up further gains in the winter and spring that carried the Red Army to the borders of Rumania, Hungary, Poland, and (in the far north) Estonia. Ukrainian peasants could now replant fields twice ravaged by scorched-earth tactics (by retreating Russians in 1941 and by retreating Germans in 1943). Relief came to Sevastopol and, at last, to Leningrad, where a million people had succumbed to bombing, shelling, and starvation.

The Red Army used the same "alternating sector" approach in this period that the French used on the Western Front in World War One and that Montgomery used at El Alamein: attack a sector, wait for the Germans to move in reinforcements, and then attack a different sector, forcing a new German scramble to reinforce. This was a retrograde strategy, a far cry from blitzkrieg, and it worked. The Germans had neither the manpower nor machines to cover the whole front, and the constant movement of units to plug gaps imposed additional wear and tear. There were also growing shortages of the 88-mm gun and the rugged Focke-Wulf (FW) 190 fighter, which were good tank destroyers that Berlin had to keep at home to ward off the Allied strategic bombers, and shortages of horses, which still transported many divisions in a Wehrmacht that was never completely motorized.

The Soviets, by contrast, fielded nearly 300 divisions and thousands of tanks and planes (and horses) and were therefore able to slog along, sector by sector, despite their own high losses. The American Lend-Lease Program provided significant help, not only food and trucks but millions of uniforms and boots that reduced human suffering and (what mattered most to Stalin) casualties from frostbite. But the real key to the victories was the Kremlin's early decision to manufacture only a few models of basic weapons in astronomical quantities. Sometimes the design was superb, as with the T34 tank and an innovative rocket launcher (called "Stalin's Organ" for its rumbling sound) that could pour a ton of explosives into the enemy lines with each discharge. Others, like the little Yak fighter planes and much artillery, were less adequate but appeared in such numbers as to neutralize the German edge in tactics and quality.

Hitler's leadership was by now poor. Although (contrary to myth) Hitler did permit his armies to retreat, he disliked giving ground and sometimes forbade it, as at Stalingrad, or delayed too long, as in the Caucasus and the Ukraine. In 1944, moreover, he became wedded to the idea of "hedgehog" urban strongpoints, a tactic that vitiated German maneuverability, still a strength, and allowed the Red Army to encircle or bypass German formations with relative ease as they drove to the edge of the Greater Reich. It did not help that two erstwhile Axis partners, Finland and Rumania, asked Stalin for terms of surrender.

Only the center of the German line, the sector bounded by the Pripet and Dvina Rivers on the approaches to Minsk, escaped more or less unscathed in early 1944. Its time would soon come.

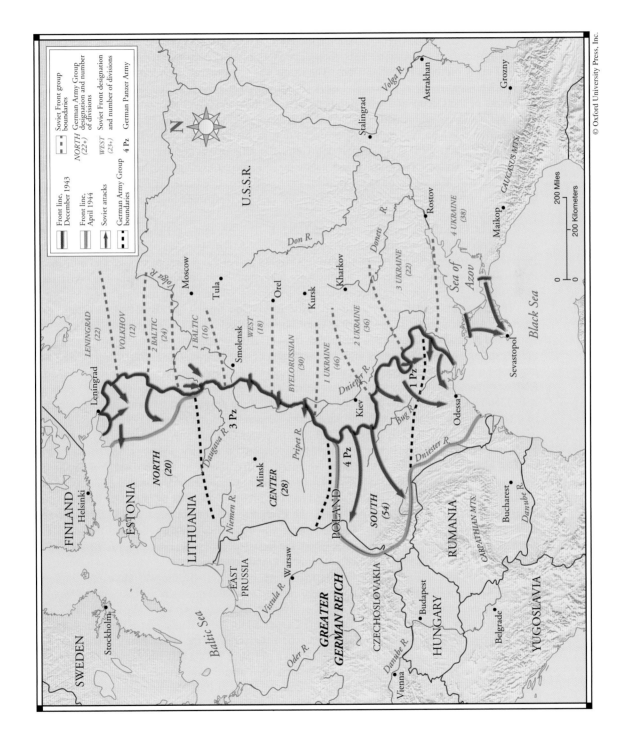

**Legend**

| | Front line, December 1943 |
| | Front line, April 1944 |
| | Soviet attacks |
| | German Army Group boundaries |

| | Soviet Front group boundaries |
| *NORTH* (22+) | German Army Group designation and number of divisions |
| *WEST* (23+) | Soviet Front designation and number of divisions |
| **4 Pz** | German Panzer Army |

SWEDEN

Stockholm

FINLAND

Helsinki

*Baltic Sea*

ESTONIA

LITHUANIA

EAST PRUSSIA

*LENINGRAD* (22)

Leningrad

*VOLKHOV* (12)

*2 BALTIC* (24)

*1 BALTIC* (16)

Moscow

Tula

*Volga R.*

U.S.S.R.

*NORTH* (20)

**3 Pz**

*Daugava R.*

*Niemen R.*

Minsk

*CENTER* (28)

Smolensk

*WEST* (18)

Orel

*BYELORUSSIAN* (30)

*Pripet R.*

Kursk

Kharkov

*Don R.*

*Donas R.*

*1 UKRAINE* (46)

*2 UKRAINE* (36)

*3 UKRAINE* (22)

Stalingrad

Astrakhan

Grozny

*CAUCASUS MTS.*

Maikop

Rostov

*4 UKRAINE* (38)

*Sea of Azov*

Sevastopol

*Black Sea*

Odessa

*Dniester R.*

*Bug R.*

*Dnieper R.*

Kiev

**4 Pz**

**1 Pz**

GREATER GERMAN REICH

Warsaw

*Vistula R.*

POLAND

*Oder R.*

CZECHOSLOVAKIA

Vienna

*Danube R.*

Budapest

HUNGARY

*SOUTH* (54)

*CARPATHIAN MTS.*

RUMANIA

Bucharest

*Danube R.*

Belgrade

YUGOSLAVIA

| 0 | | 200 Miles |
| 0 | | 200 Kilometers |

# 21 | RESISTANCE

The fall of France left its people demoralized and passive, but this did not last. Initially correct in their behavior, the Germans became more brutal and exploitative with time, and their depredations against Jews and Communists, though popular in Vichy and among the religious hierarchy, repelled many ordinary French citizens. The result was "resistance," clandestine meetings, underground publications, secret radios, and work slowdowns, that grew into "the Resistance," organized opponents of the Occupation who numbered tens of thousands by 1943 and perhaps 200,000 by 1944 and who were emblematic of stirrings elsewhere.

Several developments helped spur opposition to the Germans. Churchill set up a Special Operations Executive (SOE) to support anti-German insurgency in Europe, to "set Europe ablaze." SOE agents provided money, arms, and instructions; gathered intelligence; and encouraged sabotage. Without Allied troops on the continent, the Resistance, like bombing and the Mediterranean campaigns, was a way to fight the Nazis indirectly. In 1942 the United States established the Office of Strategic Services (OSS) to assist.

Then in 1941 the Germans invaded the U.S.S.R. This brought the European Communist parties, hitherto instructed by Stalin to avoid anti-German activity because of the 1939 Nazi-Soviet Pact, into the struggle. The Communists were a sizable part of the prewar electorate and influenced important labor unions. Parties and unions were illegal now, but the ties and habits of conspiracy remained, and Communist engagement brought tough new adherents into the fight.

There was also Charles de Gaulle, in exile in London since 1940. By 1943 de Gaulle was receiving American Lend-Lease aid, had won support in the French Empire, had fielded troops in Africa and Italy, and was known to the French from his BBC broadcasts. De Gaulle brought the various Resistance elements together under the umbrella *Comité National de la Résistance* (CNR) and harnessed it to the Allied invasion strategy. Although the Gestapo tortured many of its leaders, the CNR survived, united Resistance fighters in the *Forces Françaises de l'Intérieur* (FFI) prior to Allied landings in Normandy, and in 1944 declared itself the provisional government of France.

The Resistance was weak in absolute terms—dependent on SOE and OSS supplies, divided geographically and politically despite CNR efforts, under Gestapo surveillance, easily penetrated by double agents—yet much was accomplished. Relying on country priests, schoolteachers, and railroad station masters, the Resistance organized escape routes to Switzerland and Spain for downed Allied pilots and escaped POWs. This was easier in Vichy France than in the German zone, as was the organization of the *maquis,* armed bands with SOE links that by late 1943 forayed from bases in the hilly regions near Switzerland, the Pyrenees, and the southeast to kill Germans and blow up railroads and highways. Major sabotage was more frequent in cities and the industrial north, especially around Lyons and Paris where the Resistance hit tank, brake, radio, chemical, and other war plants as well as coal mines, oil refineries, and power stations.

The Resistance did not wreck the German army, could not win the war alone, and brought down fierce reprisals—90,000 killed, tortured, or deported; the massacre of thousand of *maquis* fighters in the southwest; and the murder of every inhabitant of Oradour-sur-Glane in central France. It was the same in Norway, where the Germans killed thousands after a Resistance fighter blew up a heavy water installation; in Poland, where they crushed the Home Army's rebellion; and in Czechoslovakia, where they annihilated the town of Lidice for the assassination of an SS leader. Only Yugoslavia, where Communist guerrillas exploited ethnic rivalries and mountainous terrain, showed real successes. But Allied bombing and the invasion of Italy also brought heavy casualties for modest results and cost vastly more. Eisenhower generously called the French Resistance the equivalent of six divisions. Everywhere, the Resistance did what conventional warfare alone could not—enable a bludgeoned people to strike back and recover its soul.

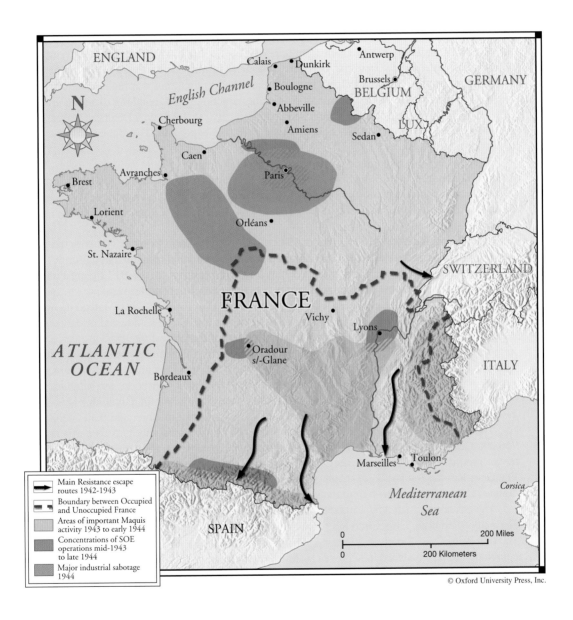

ENGLAND

English Channel

Calais
Dunkirk
Antwerp
Brussels
BELGIUM
GERMANY
LUX.

Boulogne
Abbeville
Amiens
Sedan

Cherbourg

Caen

Avranches

Brest

Paris

Orléans

SWITZERLAND

Lorient

St. Nazaire

FRANCE

Vichy

Lyons

ITALY

ATLANTIC
OCEAN

La Rochelle

Oradour
s/-Glane

Bordeaux

Marseilles
Toulon

Corsica

Mediterranean
Sea

SPAIN

N

Main Resistance escape
routes 1942-1943
Boundary between Occupied
and Unoccupied France
Areas of important Maquis
activity 1943 to early 1944
Concentrations of SOE
operations mid-1943
to late 1944
Major industrial sabotage
1944

0                    200 Miles
0          200 Kilometers

© Oxford University Press, Inc.

47

# 22 STRATEGIC BOMBING

Britain waged its strategic bombing campaign against Germany for two reasons. One was the theory that bombing would so weaken and disrupt an enemy's economy and people that the enemy would have to surrender. A second was that bombing was a way, after the evacuation of Dunkirk, to hit the enemy from a distance. It thus seemed a war-winning ("strategic") weapon and another means, along with the Resistance and the invasion of Italy, to fight Germany indirectly, on the periphery, without having to invade Northern Europe.

Churchill ordered strikes against military targets in mid-1940. But the low-flying early bombers did little damage, and the Germans shot many of them down easily. Four-engine planes such as the massive Lancaster helped, but even these had to fly at night at high elevations, which impaired accuracy. This forced a shift from specific targeting to the bombing of urban areas that crews using new navigational aids could detect at night. By 1943 Britain's Bomber Command was launching 1,000-plane raids with enough incendiaries and explosives to produce fires that could devour entire city centers.

The results were sometimes spectacular: substantial damage to Ruhr industrial towns, 40,000 dead at Hamburg, major destruction in Berlin. But firestorms were difficult to ignite in Germany's stone cities, and the Germans improved their radar, added antiaircraft guns and night fighters, and downed or damaged thousands of bombers. In late 1943 the Bomber Command's campaign slowed out of self-preservation.

The United States entered the fight in 1942, making flights from British bases with the goal of destroying key industrial facilities. This required precision bombing, meaning daylight runs, which made the planes vulnerable. The Americans hoped to compensate with the B17 Flying Fortress, a rugged four-engine bomber bristling with heavy machine guns. But factories were hard to spot even after the introduction of an electronic bombsight, and the B17s proved unable to defend themselves. In a 300-plane attack on ball-bearing plants in Schweinfurt, the Germans downed or damaged half the planes, and high losses persisted until the deployment in late 1943 of the P51 Mustang, a superb long-range fighter capable of escorting bombers to eastern Germany and decimating the Luftwaffe interceptors. With the enemy thus challenged, Bomber Command resumed its night runs. In the spring of 1944, both services focused on disrupting fuel and transportation supplies to the Normandy area. The Americans continued to target oil facilities, except for a three-day U.S.–British assault on Dresden in February 1945 that produced a raging firestorm and more than 50,000 dead.

The big bombers dropped 2 million tons of bombs on Germany and its Axis partners, killed 750,000 Germans, interdicted rail lines, choked off gasoline supplies, and forced the Reich to scatter its production facilities and keep its planes and antiaircraft batteries at home rather than in France or Russia. But it did not shatter German morale, and German military and industrial output climbed until a few months before the surrender.

The casualties, including 150,000 French and Italian civilians and 100,000 foreign workers in Germany, were high. Even Churchill fretted at the hatred this might sow in postwar Europe. About 100,000 British and American air crew died, and the campaign soaked up money (20 percent of the combined military budgets), manpower, materials, and creativity that might have gone elsewhere— for more U.S. landing craft, more and better British tanks, additional warships, and better Resistance support.

Resistance proponents claimed they could have done as much with fewer friendly (or Axis civilian) casualties. Postwar service analysts cast doubt on the bombing campaign's efficacy, but much of this criticism is hindsight. Bomber advocates overpromised, and the Allies bombed partly because at the time they could do little else. The bombing death total of roughly a million was in any case lower than the Germans inflicted during the single siege of Leningrad.

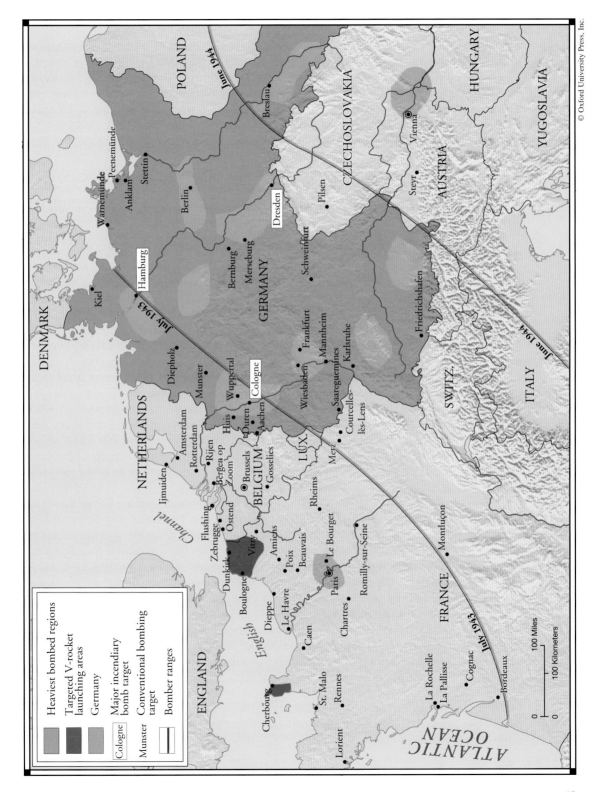

**Legend:**

Heaviest bombed regions

Targeted V-rocket launching areas

Germany

Cologne — Major incendiary bomb target

Munster — Conventional bombing target

Bomber ranges

**Place names:**

POLAND

June 1944

Peenemünde

Warnemünde

Anklam

Stettin

Breslau

Berlin

CZECHOSLOVAKIA

Vienna

Pilsen

Steyr

AUSTRIA

HUNGARY

YUGOSLAVIA

Dresden

Bernburg

Merseburg

Schweinfurt

GERMANY

Friedrichshafen

Hamburg

Kiel

July 1943

DENMARK

Diepholz

Munster

Wuppertal

Cologne

Frankfurt

Mannheim

Karlsruhe

Saarguemines

June 1944

SWITZ.

ITALY

NETHERLANDS

Amsterdam

Rotterdam

Bergen op Zoom

Ijmuiden

Huis

Duren

Aachen

Wiesbaden

Courcelles-les-Lens

LUX.

Metz

BELGIUM

Brussels

Gosselies

Rheims

Flushing

Zebrugge

Ostend

Dunkirk

Boulogne

Vitry

Amiens

Poix

Beauvais

Le Bourget

Romilly-sur-Seine

Montluçon

Channel

English Channel

Dieppe

Le Havre

Caen

Chartres

Paris

FRANCE

July 1943

Cherbourg

St. Malo

Rennes

Lorient

La Rochelle

La Pallisse

Cognac

Bordeaux

ENGLAND

ATLANTIC OCEAN

0      100 Miles

0      100 Kilometers

# 23 | ITALY

At the Casablanca Conference in January 1943, Roosevelt argued for a landing in German-held France that summer. Churchill urged action in Italy or the Balkans. They compromised on Sicily. The invasion of Sicily began in July with an attack by 160,000 American, British, and Canadian troops supported by 4,000 aircraft and powerful naval forces. The British 8th Army under Montgomery landed unopposed near Syracusa and moved north before bogging down against German units around Mt. Etna. The American 5th Army under George Patton landed at Gela, fought off Axis counterattacks, and moved (against orders) to take Palermo and Messina, arriving in August ahead of Montgomery.

The invasion was a partial success. The Allies gained experience in amphibious operations, prompted the Fascist Grand Council to depose Mussolini and start surrender talks, and secured the island. But they failed to keep 100,000 German and Italian soldiers from escaping with 10,000 vehicles to the mainland.

Churchill now urged an invasion of Italy, which he asserted was Europe's "soft underbelly," to draw Wehrmacht formations from Russia (and allow the 8th Army to win a victory). Roosevelt proposed a landing in southern France but capitulated to placate his air chiefs, who wanted bomber bases in Italy. The invasion commenced in September 1943. Montgomery took Reggio and and Taranto and moved smartly up the right side of Italy's "boot" to Foggia. The Americans landed at Salerno on the left and moved against Naples. But Germany, deciding that Italy's mountains and rivers favored its defense, committed 16 divisions and constructed two formidable defensive lines, the Gustav Line above Naples and the Gothic Line north of Rome. The Allied advance slowed to a crawl.

In January 1944 the United States landed at Anzio to try to outflank the Germans at the Gustav Line but failed to exploit the beachhead. In February Allied bombers pounded the ancient Abbey of Monte Cassino in a vain effort to breach the line. Not until May did the Allies break through, whereupon the American general Mark Clark sent his troops from Anzio north to capture Rome rather than east to trap the retreating Germans, who escaped again. By the time the Allied advance resumed that fall, it was raining and divisions were being withdrawn to support operations in France. The Allies punctured the Gothic Line only in April 1945—two weeks before the end of the war.

The battle for Italy drew some German divisions and Luftwaffe squadrons from Russia and France. German casualties were high, especially in the final days. The Italian government switched sides. However, although the campaign removed an Axis power from the war, the Allies lost 300,000 dead and wounded, and many of the wounds were crippling—blindness from flying rock and trenchfoot from the world's worst mud. The biggest bombing attack from Italy, on Rumanian oil fields, was a disaster. The destruction of Monte Cassino produced only ill will.

Command reputations suffered—Montgomery's for pettiness and inability to exploit, Clark's for poor judgment and glory-mongering. Monty did orchestrate another large multinational army that included Poles and Canadians, who proved capable and valiant, and the Free French, who were preparing for the liberation of their homeland. Unlike the Americans, Montgomery also worked well with the partisan guerrillas of Italy. Eisenhower relieved Patton, a brilliant but hot-tempered martinet, for slapping and cursing shell-shocked soldiers at two field hospitals.

Italy was not a "soft underbelly"; it was what a British soldier called a "tough old gut." George Marshall, U.S. Army Chief of Staff, termed it an "expensive sideshow," and it stoked American suspicions that Britain preferred imperial adventures in the Mediterranean to bearding the Nazi lion across the Channel in its den.

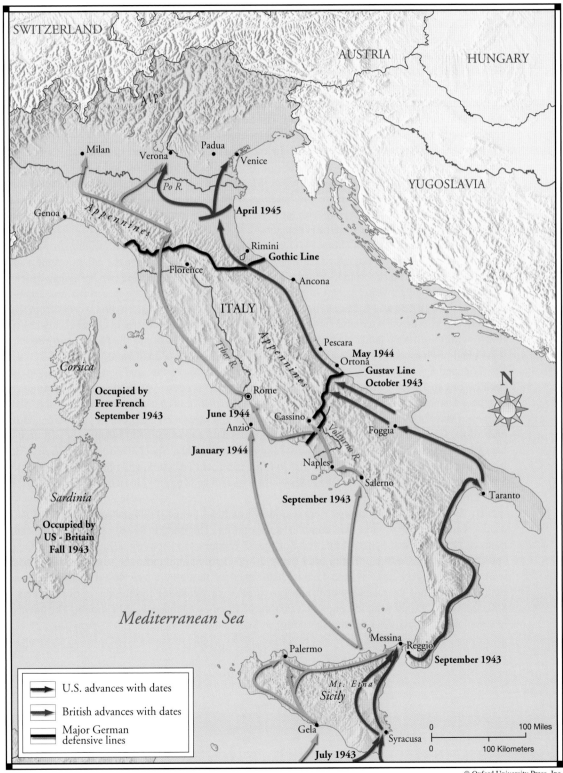

SWITZERLAND

AUSTRIA

HUNGARY

*Alps*

Milan

Verona

Padua

Venice

*Po R.*

YUGOSLAVIA

Genoa

*Appennines*

**April 1945**

Rimini

**Gothic Line**

Florence

Ancona

ITALY

*Corsica*

*Tiber R.*

*Appennines*

Pescara

**May 1944**

Ortona

**Gustav Line**

**October 1943**

Rome

**June 1944**

Anzio

Cassino

*Volturno R.*

Foggia

**Occupied by
Free French
September 1943**

**January 1944**

Naples

Salerno

*Sardinia*

**Occupied by
US - Britain
Fall 1943**

**September 1943**

Taranto

**September 1943**

*Mediterranean Sea*

Messina

Reggio

Palermo

*Mt. Etna*

*Sicily*

**N**

| | |
|---|---|
| → | U.S. advances with dates |
| → | British advances with dates |
| ▬ | Major German defensive lines |

Gela

Syracusa

0    100 Miles

0    100 Kilometers

**July 1943**

# 24 OPERATION OVERLORD—THE NORMANDY INVASION

Long criticized by Stalin for not relieving the pressure on the U.S.S.R. by invading northern Europe, Roosevelt and even Churchill, who favored peripheral campaigns, understood from the start that an invasion of France would ultimately be necessary to defeat Germany. Planning for a cross-Channel operation began in 1942 and accelerated with the Mediterranean successes of 1943. The Italian campaign faltered partly because the Americans insisted on concentrating troops and materials in England for a Channel crossing. The Soviets launched a huge mid-1944 ground assault against the Germans partly to facilitate the Anglo-American landings.

Operation Overlord was in fact one of the most carefully planned and spectacularly successful military operations in history. An elaborate ruse involving General Patton and a phantom army in Britain confused Berlin as to the probable landing site, leaving Normandy defenses thin and Hitler reluctant to commit reserves even as the landings were occurring. The British and Canadians ran into important panzer divisions, but even these were only accidentally in position while resting and refitting from fighting on the Eastern Front.

The Allied beach targets (Map 24A) conformed to the areas of troop buildup in Southern England, which in turn reflected the fact that the American area was close to the Atlantic approaches for the U.S. soldiers and equipment required to assault Fortress Europe. The two American beaches were on the Atlantic (western) end of the invasion area across from the American embarkation ports; the three British and Canadian beaches were on the European (eastern) end, across from their respective ports. Beach assignments in turn largely determined the paths of advance toward the Reich, with the British and Canadians moving north along the coast and the Americans sweeping inland and north to avoid crossing the supply lines of their Anglo-Canadian allies.

The landings on June 6 were a masterpiece of amphibious warfare and combined arms, in part because of experience gained in the Mediterranean theater. Predawn air drops on either end of the beachhead area helped sow confusion and prevent German flanking maneuvers. Precision naval gunnery (Map 24B) helped reduce German seaward gun emplacements. Destroyers screened the ends of the Channel to prevent U-boat penetrations. Allied air power kept the skies largely free of Luftwaffe fighters, already scarce from losses in Russia and Italy. Specialized landing craft ferried troops and equipment (from telephone wire to filing cabinets to mortars) and provided covering fire. Specialized tanks (with flails to explode land mines, carpet rolls to provide traction on sand, and the like) supported the landings.

By day's end, 125,000 troops were ashore. Casualties—some 9,000, fewer than half of them dead—were light for so large and complex an operation. The biggest losses came in the morning hours at Omaha Beach, where Americans of the 1st Infantry Division, the famed "Big Red One," encountered crack German infantry after being dropped prematurely into the surf. But the invaders were onshore to stay, and by June 12 they had linked up in a continuous 40-mile beachhead that both permitted full lateral movement and provided a narrow space for further reinforcements— 850,000 men, 150,000 vehicles, and 600,000 tons of supplies by the end of the month. The advance toward Caen, Bayeux, St.-Lô, and Cherbourg was on.

## A. D-Day Landings

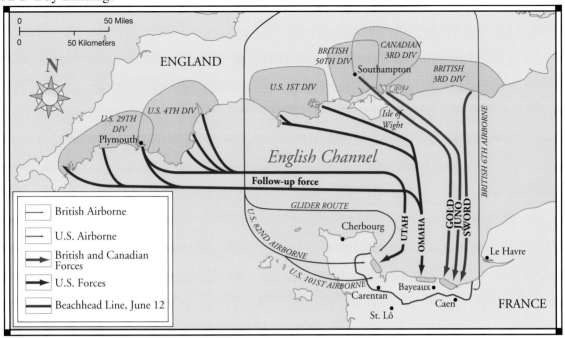

## B.  Naval Bombardment Patterns

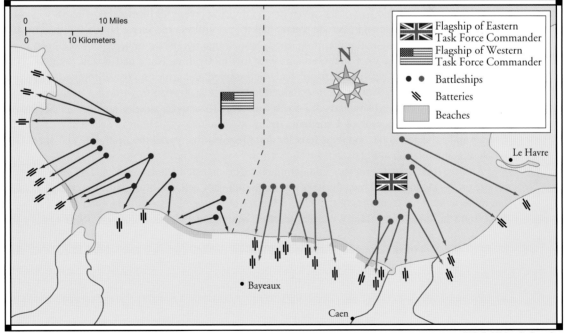

# 25 | THE ALLIED ADVANCE

With their beaches secured and linked, the Allies had two goals: for the Americans, to seize the Cotentin Peninsula and the harbor of Cherbourg, thereby securing a supply route; for the British and Canadians, to take the city of Caen, thereby pushing the beachhead inland.

Neither advance went smoothly. On the Cotentin, the U.S. forces battled throughout late June against marshy ground, impenetrable peasant hedgerows, and four German infantry divisions. It took three weeks to reach Cherbourg, where the Germans had wrecked the harbor. Not till August did supplies start to trickle through. Three panzer divisions meanwhile kept Montgomery's forces from moving past Caen into open country, despite heavy RAF bombing. Monty regrouped; in order to keep German units from heading toward Cotentin against the Americans, he then renewed the attack before faltering against German Tiger tanks.

But the push toward Caen kept enough German armor busy to allow the United States, after unleashing the heaviest aerial and artillery bombardment of the campaign, to take the strategically positioned town of St.-Lô. On August 1 the United States formed the 3rd Army, gave it to George Patton, and told him to break rapidly around the German left and then northeast in a sweeping arc south of the German lines.

At almost the same time, Hitler sent armored formations westward toward the village of Mortain in a counterattack designed to shatter a U.S. position that looked overextended. The counterattack failed, and now the Germans themselves were overextended and in danger of being trapped in a giant pocket by U.S. troops and Montgomery's forces, which had finally broken through at Caen. Thus developed the largest armored encounter of the Western Front, the Battle of the Falaise Pocket, a "cauldron" fight that Allied superiority in guns and planes turned into a major victory. The east end of the pocket proved hard to close and 50,000 Germans escaped, but they left 50,000 others behind, with thousands of horses and nearly all their equipment. The way to northern France lay suddenly open.

Overall Allied casualties reached tens of thousands during the push inland. The sheer size of the contending armies (2 million men by late August) was a factor. So was their character. Half of the German divisions and five of the seven panzer divisions were SS formations. The SS was originally Hitler's bodyguard and assassin squad, and the SS still ran the secret police and the concentration camps. But it also had a Waffen (armed) branch that by 1944 numbered 900,000 men in 38 divisions. Many of these were non-Germans with low motivation. But a half-dozen, some of them in Normandy, were the best the Germans had, well trained and armed and swelling with Nazi zeal and cruelty: The 1st SS Panzer Division shredded a British formation west of Caen, the 2nd SS Panzer Division murdered hundreds of French following Resistance attacks, and the 12th SS Panzer Division murdered hundreds of Canadians trying to surrender near Juno Beach. They gave little quarter and expected none, and their ferocity and firepower increased the death rate and staved off wholesale annihilation at Falaise.

And they generated ferocious counterattacks. The untested Canadian teenagers who stormed ashore on D-Day lost 3,000 men the next week and more at Caen, mainly against the equally untried but more murderous teenagers of the 12th SS Panzer Division. Yet it was the Canadians who struggled south in jerry-built infantry carriers to close the gap at Falaise, killing an SS general in the process and taking few prisoners. And men from Poland, refugee veterans from 1939 now organized as the 1st Polish Armored Division and ashore under Montgomery, helped the Canadians. After many of the fleeing Germans had escaped, a Polish lieutenant linked up with an American soldier to close the Falaise gap, and Poles with a blood debt to repay the Reich held it shut. Canadian soldiers later raised a simple marker near 325 Polish graves at the Falaise gap that read "A Polish Battlefield."

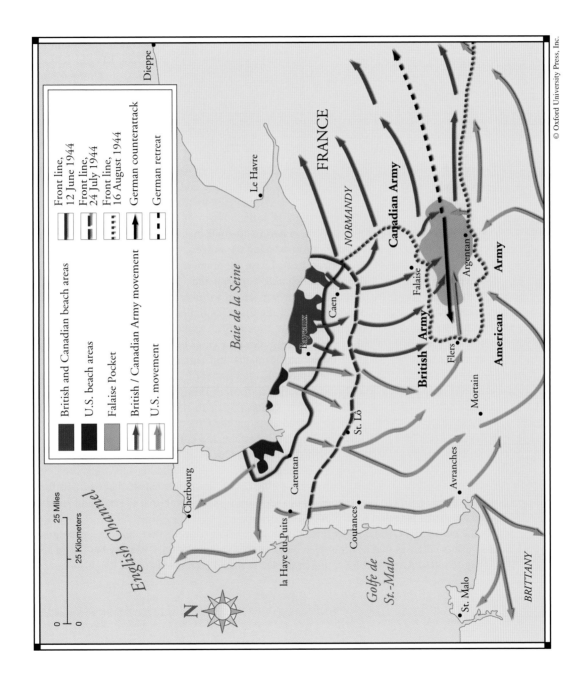

**Legend**

- British and Canadian beach areas
- U.S. beach areas
- Falaise Pocket
- British / Canadian Army movement
- U.S. movement
- Front line, 12 June 1944
- Front line, 24 July 1944
- Front line, 16 August 1944
- German counterattack
- German retreat

English Channel

25 Miles

25 Kilometers

N

Dieppe

Le Havre

FRANCE

NORMANDY

Baie de la Seine

Cherbourg

Carentan

Bayeux

Caen

Canadian Army

Falaise

Argentan

British Army

American Army

Flers

Mortain

St. Lô

la Haye du Puits

Coutances

Golfe de St.-Malo

Avranches

St. Malo

BRITTANY

# 26 | THE BATTLE OF WHITE RUSSIA

The success of the Normandy landings owed something to valor, something to meticulous planning, and something to Resistance sabotage, strategic bombing, and Allied pressure in Italy. But Normandy also succeeded because the bulk of German firepower was on the Eastern Front confronting what the Russians called Operation Bagration, or the Battle for White Russia (Byelorussia), a massive Soviet campaign that resulted in what historian John Keegan calls one of the "greatest defeats" ever inflicted in war—the destruction of Germany's Army Group Center.

The campaign was striking for many reasons. First, it was a summer campaign. Until late 1943 the Germans virtually owned the summer and therefore the campaign initiative on the Eastern Front. By 1944 the Soviets owned the summer.

Second, Soviet production of tanks, rockets, guns, and planes was now so immense that the Red Army could equip some 500 divisions and support them with 9,000 armored vehicles. The strongest and best of these faced Army Group Center, to which Adolph Hitler had given the thankless responsibility of defending Minsk, Warsaw, East Prussia, and the Fatherland itself.

Third, so powerful were the Soviets vis-à-vis their foe that they could partially disregard the tactics of encirclement and envelopment and the refined forms of armored blitzkrieg. Instead, they not only drove into the German flanks from north and south but also attacked straight ahead into the very nose of the Wehrmacht positions, producing the biggest "cauldron" battle of the war.

Fourth, the impact of the American Lend-Lease Program was now evident. The Russians in 1944 moved across huge distances, comparable to those the Germans had traversed in 1941, because they transported their infantry, always essential to protect tanks and artillery, with U.S. trucks. The Soviets had vast firepower, and for the first time in history, they were enjoying the full fruits of the internal combustion engine.

Fifth, the Russians not only shattered Army Group Center but moved 300 miles through the Baltic states in the north and 500 miles into Rumania and Hungary in the south. This removed German Axis partners from the war and precluded the possibility of a German flanking attack. It also established an unassailable Russian position in Eastern Europe when the war ended.

Two further points are worth noting in connection with the postwar settlement. First, the Soviets did not move into Yugoslavia, instead allowing the Communist partisan leader Josip Broz Tito to take control, inadvertently enabling him to establish a certain postwar independence from the Kremlin. Second, the Red Army halted east of Warsaw even though resistance fighters of the Polish Home Army fomented an armed uprising to coincide with the Soviet approach. The Germans proceeded to massacre the Poles before retreating. Some military analysts believe that the Red Army had to halt in order to resupply, but Cold War historians note that the halt and subsequent massacre crushed a potential source of anti-Soviet opposition.

By the end of 1944, some 38 German divisions had been ripped apart, leaving a gaping hole in Hitler's eastern defenses that he scrambled desperately to plug. Not only Warsaw but Berlin seemed to lie open to a Red Army that by spring at the latest would be reprovisioned.

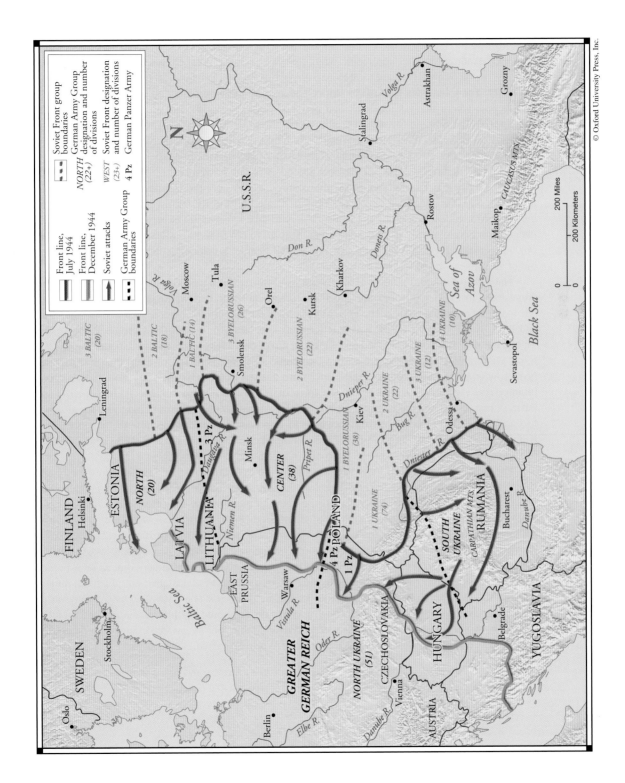

**Legend:**

Front line, July 1944

Front line, December 1944

Soviet attacks

German Army Group boundaries

Soviet Front group boundaries

German Army Group designation and number of divisions — NORTH (22+)

Soviet Front designation and number of divisions — WEST (23+)

German Panzer Army — 4 Pz

N

SWEDEN

Oslo

Stockholm

FINLAND

Helsinki

Baltic Sea

Leningrad

ESTONIA

LATVIA

LITHUANIA

NORTH (20)

3 Pz

3 BALTIC (20)

2 BALTIC (18)

1 BALTIC (14)

Daugava R.

Niemen R.

EAST PRUSSIA

Warsaw

Vistula R.

GREATER GERMAN REICH

Berlin

Elbe R.

Oder R.

Minsk

CENTER (38)

Pripet R.

3 BYELORUSSIAN (26)

2 BYELORUSSIAN (22)

1 BYELORUSSIAN (38)

Smolensk

Moscow

Tula

Orel

Kursk

Kharkov

U.S.S.R.

Volga R.

Don R.

Donets R.

Stalingrad

Astrakhan

Rostov

Sea of Azov

CAUCASUS MTS.

Maikop

Grozny

Black Sea

Sevastopol

4 Pz

1 Pz

POLAND

NORTH UKRAINE (51)

CZECHOSLOVAKIA

Vienna

Danube R.

AUSTRIA

HUNGARY

Belgrade

YUGOSLAVIA

SOUTH UKRAINE

CARPATHIAN MTS.

RUMANIA

Bucharest

Danube R.

Odessa

Dniester R.

Bug R.

Dnieper R.

Kiev

1 UKRAINE (74)

2 UKRAINE (22)

3 UKRAINE (12)

4 UKRAINE (10)

0    200 Miles

0    200 Kilometers

# 27 THE LIBERATION OF FRANCE

Following the victory at the Falaise pocket, the Allies moved in dramatic leaps for the first time since landing on the continent. Montgomery's armies brushed aside makeshift German defenses on the Seine River and took Rouen on August 30 and Amiens, 150 miles from Falaise, two days later. The Canadians split off to isolate and capture the well-defended Channel ports (including Dieppe, where many Canadians had perished in a 1942 raid). British and American armies drove across the Somme toward Belgium, taking the great port city of Antwerp, much prized by Eisenhower, on September 3. The Germans still held the north bank of Antwerp's Scheldt Estuary, however, so the port itself remained unusable, a major blow to Allied logistics until commandos and bomber crews demolished the last German defenders in late November.

Plunging past Paris, Patton's 3$^{rd}$ Army captured Nancy near the frontier on September 16. To the south, 500,000 American and French troops landed on the Riviera in mid-August, seized the harbor of Marseilles, headed up the Rhone Valley to take Lyons and Dijon, and linked up with elements from Patton's army in mid-September. This drive covered 400 miles in six weeks, captured 60,000 Germans for 7,000 U.S.–French losses, and opened a valuable supply line before running out of steam near the Mosel in October.

The sweep through France was partly the result of the weakness of the Germans, who by late August had lost 600,000 troops and much equipment and who had no air support. But it was also due to Allied arms and tactics. The U.S. M4 Sherman tanks, built to General Patton's specifications and used by all Western allies, had smaller guns and less armor than the German Panthers and Tigers, but they were quicker, used less fuel, and broke down less often, meaning better pursuit and fewer vulnerable stops. And there were vast numbers of them, enough of them that, once free of hedgerow country, they produced the 5 to 1 ratio needed to kill a Tiger. They also enjoyed good infantry and especially air support in the form of B26s and the redoubtable P47s, superb "tank busters" that devastated the German formations. By August the Americans could radio for close air and artillery strikes to take out strongholds or to stop counterattacks and know the support would be there in good weather, an example of the combined arms operations that were once the preserve of Germany alone but were now the hallmark of its enemies.

The Americans bypassed Paris because Patton did not want to tie up his tanks in the city and Eisenhower did not want to feed it. This left the initiative to the local Resistance organization, which desperately wanted to fight against the German garrison the way Resistance fighters elsewhere were, whether they were members of Charles de Gaulle's armies or the Fighting French of the Interior, who helped during the southern landings and in the clearing of Brittany. But de Gaulle worried that the Paris movement had too many Communists and that urban fighting would destroy the city. He persuaded Ike, who liked him better than other U.S. commanders did, to let a French armored division from Normandy liberate the city. In the end the Resistance did not spark a mass uprising (it rang church bells instead), and the Germans did not resist. On August 25 General de Gaulle marched with his battalions through the Arc de Triomphe, rallied his nation, and won the support he would need to demand a seat at the victors' table. For every free country, the liberation of Paris was one of the most dramatic moments of World War Two.

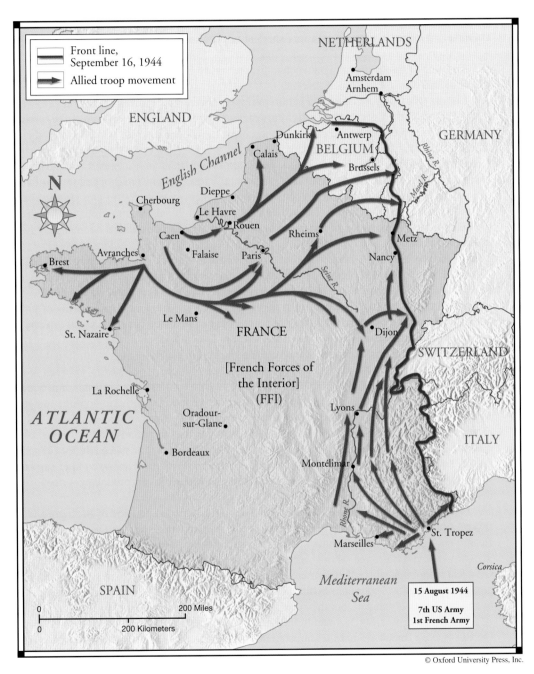

Front line,
September 16, 1944

Allied troop movement

NETHERLANDS

Amsterdam
Arnhem

ENGLAND

Dunkirk
Calais
*English Channel*
Dieppe
Le Havre
Cherbourg
Rouen
Rheims
Caen
Avranches
Falaise
Paris
Brest
Le Mans
St. Nazaire

GERMANY

Antwerp
BELGIUM
Brussels
*Rhine R.*
*Mosel R.*
Metz
Nancy

*Seine R.*

FRANCE

[French Forces of
the Interior]
(FFI)

Dijon

SWITZERLAND

La Rochelle
Oradour-
sur-Glane

ATLANTIC
OCEAN

Lyons

ITALY

Bordeaux

Montélimar

*Rhône R.*

St. Tropez

Marseilles

Corsica

SPAIN

*Mediterranean
Sea*

15 August 1944

7th US Army
1st French Army

0        200 Miles
0        200 Kilometers

N

© Oxford University Press, Inc.

# 28 THE BATTLE OF THE BULGE

By fall 1944, the western Allies' advance had ground down in the old pattern. On the one hand, the Germans shortened their lines of communication as they fell back toward the Fatherland, which meant they could reinforce and rearm more easily. On the other hand, the Allied supply columns got longer. Every division was short of fuel as it approached the Rhine, and many lacked ammunition. Not even round-the-clock truck convoys from Normandy and Marseilles could provide gasoline to troops operating at such a distance on so broad a front, in part because the supply trucks themselves used so much gasoline.

Eisenhower therefore decreed a halt to resupply. That did not sit well with Montgomery on the left or Patton on the right, each of whom urged a narrow thrust in his own sector; Ike turned them down. But in September he did permit Montgomery to mount a complicated operation that would utilize precision air drops and rapid tank movements to seize eight bridges leading to Arnhem in the Netherlands, from which Monty's forces would cross the Rhine and turn east for Berlin. Almost everything in Operation Market Garden went wrong: Paratroopers were dropped too far from their targets, an undetected SS panzer division covered Arnhem, a huge traffic jam slowed the Allied tanks, fog grounded the planes. The Allies ended up with a salient into Holland that they later exploited during the invasion of Germany, but they lost 10,000 men and left Arnhem and the Rhine in German hands.

At the same time, American forces experienced a bitter setback attempting to secure the Hurtgen Forest, a wooded region just over the German border that seemed to be a threat to a future U.S. advance. The Hurtgen was not an important objective; historian Stephen Ambrose even calls the plan to take it "stupid." The Germans had filled the forest with a murderous array of pillboxes, barbed wire, land mines, and machine-gun nests; foliage prevented accurate Allied artillery fire or air attacks. The Americans finally cleared the forest in December, but they lost 25,000 men (the better part of four divisions) doing it. Farther to the right, Patton lost more men by hurling them against strongholds in the Metz area.

These multiple losses, the products of a command carelessness not confined to any one nationality, set up the last major German offensive of the war, devised by Hitler to do three things: overwhelm the weakened Allied front opposite the Ardennes, take Antwerp and cut the Allied supply chain, and trigger a crisis in the Allied high command that might wreck the Anglo-American alliance. Thus unfolded the Battle of the Bulge in late December, a time when Hitler believed, accurately, that bad weather would minimize Allied air strikes. The attack achieved total surprise, and within a week the Germans were a few miles from the Meuse River, producing a deep salient in the front.

Inside the bulge, however, U.S. forces held on to the key road junction of Bastogne, damaging several German divisions and posing a threat to the panzer flanks, and on December 23 the skies cleared enough for planes to pound the German supply lines. Two days later, elements of Patton's 3rd Army relieved Bastogne. Shortly afterward Hitler authorized a withdrawal, By mid-January the Germans were back where they started, except that they had left 100,000 men and nearly all their precious tanks, guns, and planes behind. The Allies had also lost 100,000 (dead, wounded, or frostbitten) and much armament, but they could replace these; Germany could not.

The Allied drive from Normandy thus had five distinct phases. The first four were success on D-Day, buildup, breakout and the pursuit across France, and failure to breach the frontier culminating in the Battle of the Bulge. But the Reich had expended its last reserves. The Allies now gathered themselves for the crossing of the Rhine and the conquest of Western Germany, the fifth and final phase of the advance and its crowning success.

## A. Fall Allied Operations

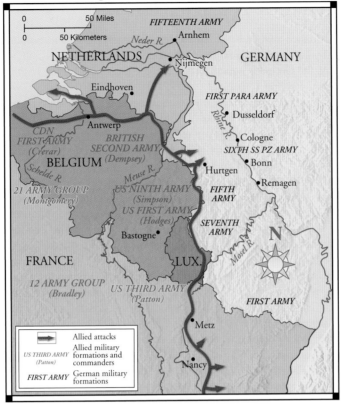

*FIFTEENTH ARMY*

*Neder R.*

Arnhem

NETHERLANDS

GERMANY

Nijmegen

Eindhoven

*FIRST PARA ARMY*

Dusseldorf

*Rhine R.*

Antwerp

Cologne

CDN FIRST ARMY
(Crerar)

*BRITISH SECOND ARMY*
*(Dempsey)*

*SIXTH SS PZ ARMY*

BELGIUM

Bonn

*Schelde R.*

*Meuse R.*

Hurtgen

Remagen

21 ARMY GROUP
(Montgomery)

US NINTH ARMY
(Simpson)

*FIFTH ARMY*

US FIRST ARMY
(Hodges)

*SEVENTH ARMY*

Bastogne

N

FRANCE

LUX.

*Mosel R.*

12 ARMY GROUP
(Bradley)

US THIRD ARMY
(Patton)

*FIRST ARMY*

Metz

0 — 50 Miles
0 — 50 Kilometers

Nancy

→ Allied attacks

*US THIRD ARMY (Patton)* — Allied military formations and commanders

*FIRST ARMY* — German military formations

## B. Battle of the Bulge

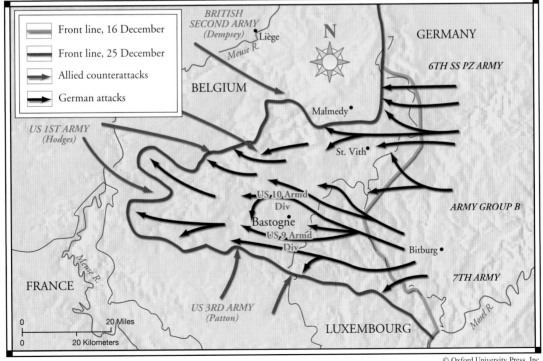

═══ Front line, 16 December

━━━ Front line, 25 December

➤ Allied counterattacks

➤ German attacks

*BRITISH SECOND ARMY*
*(Dempsey)*

Liège

GERMANY

*Meuse R.*

N

*6TH SS PZ ARMY*

BELGIUM

Malmedy

*US 1ST ARMY*
*(Hodges)*

St. Vith

US 10 Armd Div

*ARMY GROUP B*

Bastogne

US 9 Armd Div

Bitburg

*7TH ARMY*

*Meuse R.*

*US 3RD ARMY*
*(Patton)*

LUXEMBOURG

*Mosel R.*

0 — 20 Miles
0 — 20 Kilometers

© Oxford University Press, Inc.

61

# 29 | THE DEFEAT OF NAZI GERMANY

The Grand Alliance shattered the Third Reich in early 1945, but only after difficult fighting. Weakened by air attacks, the failure of the December Ardennes assault, and the hammer blows of the Red Army, the Germans nonetheless remained a resourceful foe requiring four more bloody months to subdue.

The Russians began these final battles with direct assaults from the north through East Prussia and straight west through Poland toward Berlin. Remembering the Wehrmacht's rapine and pillage in the east and commanding 15,000 armored vehicles, Stalin's armies showed little mercy, killing thousands of German soldiers attempting to surrender, driving hordes of German civilians (many newly settled on Polish soil) into the winter elements, and, as ill-disciplined rear-guard Red Army elements arrived in the Reich cities, raping German women of all ages.

German army remnants, being commanded by loyalists such as Guderian and benefiting from Nazi zeal and shortened lines of communication, resisted fiercely and even launched a counter-attack from the Baltic area north of Berlin that temporarily halted the Red tank columns, ever concerned, like all ground forces, with protecting their lengthening flanks. But there was no stopping the Soviet juggernaut.

Just as the Battle of White Russia facilitated the Normandy landings, the exploits of the huge Western armies, with their fleets of tanks and trucks and total air supremacy, now facilitated the Soviet victories. The Canadians and British cleared the coastal areas, which opened additional Atlantic ports, halted the last launches of the unmanned V1 and V2 rockets that killed 15,000 British in the last year of the war, and saved thousands of Dutch and Danes from death by starvation and reprisal.

The American 1st and 9th Armies crossed the Rhine in early March, encircled the Ruhr industrial region, and accepted the surrender of 400,000 hungry, ill-equipped, poorly commanded German soldiers—the largest Axis capitulation of the war—before moving past the Harz Mountains to the Elbe River. Patton's 3rd Army moved northeast and then, to forestall a rumored German retreat into a mountain "redoubt" veered sharply southeastward along the edge of the mountains of western Czechoslovakia to the city of Linz, Hitler's home town, which was occupied on May 5. In this drive Patton's forces crossed seven major rivers, demonstrating a fording skill matched only by the Red Army.

The U.S. 7th Army, which had landed in Southern France in mid-August, moved up to protect Patton's southern flank and occupy Bavaria, including both Nuremberg, site of the great Nazi party rallies of the 1930s, and Munich, where Hitler had failed to seize power in the "Beer-Hall Putsch" of 1923. The 5th Army finally fought its way at enormous cost through German defenses in Italy to meet 7th Army elements at the Brenner Pass, a key access route to Austria. By now, too, the French 1st Army was a significant force, fielding seven divisions, providing additional Allied firepower and occupation capacity, and, most critical to Charles de Gaulle, guaranteeing a presence in postwar occupied Germany.

Though perfectly willing to bomb and shell recalcitrant German towns, Western troops on the whole dealt lightly with the defeated Reich citizenry once the fighting stopped, particularly in the villages, where people were eager to please the young conquerors and where appearances seemed not unlike, say, the American Midwest.

Others were discovering things about the Reich that shook them to the core of their being.

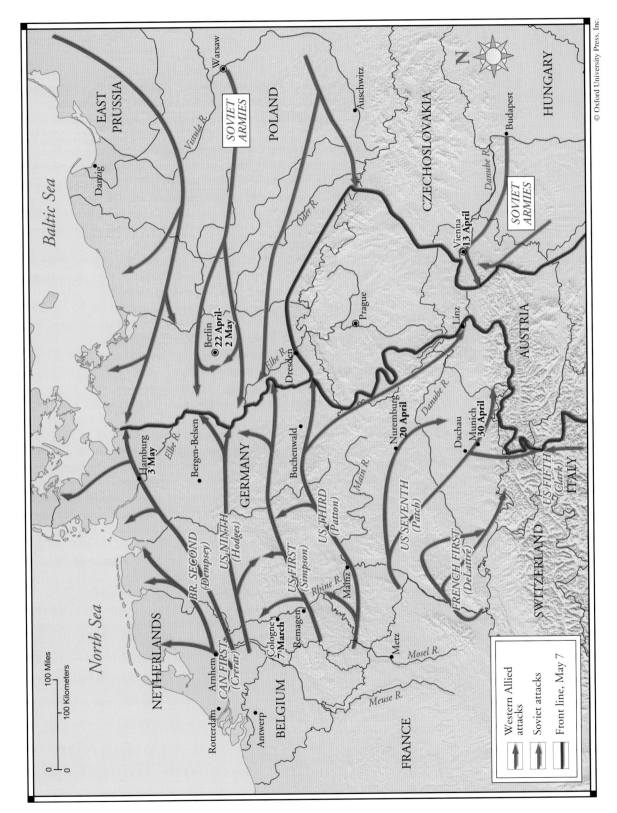

© Oxford University Press, Inc.

Baltic Sea

EAST
PRUSSIA

Danzig

Warsaw

*SOVIET
ARMIES*

POLAND

Vistula R.

Oder R.

Auschwitz

CZECHOSLOVAKIA

HUNGARY

Budapest

Danube R.

*SOVIET
ARMIES*

Vienna
**13 April**

Linz

AUSTRIA

Prague

Berlin
**22 April-
2 May**

Elbe R.

Dresden

Nuremburg
**20 April**

Danube R.

Dachau

Munich
**30 April**

Hamburg
**3 May**

Bergen-Belsen

GERMANY

Buchenwald

Elbe R.

Main R.

SWITZERLAND

US FIFTH
(Clark)

ITALY

North Sea

*BR. SECOND*
(Dempsey)

*US NINTH*
(Hodges)

*US FIRST*
(Simpson)

Rhine R.

Mainz

*US THIRD*
(Patton)

*US SEVENTH*
(Patch)

*FRENCH FIRST*
(DeLatre)

NETHERLANDS

Arnhem

CAN FIRST
(Crerar)

Cologne
**7 March**

Remagen

Metz

Mosel R.

Rotterdam

Antwerp

BELGIUM

Meuse R.

FRANCE

100 Miles

100 Kilometers

0
0

N

Western Allied
attacks

Soviet attacks

Front line, May 7

# 30 THE FALL OF BERLIN

In the aftermath of their great summer offensive of 1944, the Soviets drove to the east bank of the Oder River and into Hitler's East European satellites of Hungary, Austria, and Czechoslovakia. The Red Army now deployed nearly 15,000 tanks and armored vehicles and an equal number of aircraft against Germany, which was also fighting (and killing) Americans and British in the west. The stage was set for the clash over Berlin, capital of what the Russians termed the "fascist beast."

Berlin lay within the Russian sphere, as determined (in accordance with earlier suggestions by Churchill) at the Yalta Conference in February 1945. This was one reason Eisenhower declined to send Allied soldiers into the city. He also thought it would cost him 100,000 men, an estimate that turned out to be too low. The Germans, though without air power, had a small defensive perimeter, short lines of communication, rabid Nazi loyalists on the ground, and a ruined city to hide in that sheltered the command bunker of Adolf Hitler himself. Ike willingly relinquished responsibility for conquering Berlin to Stalin, who eagerly accepted it.

Fearful as always of incursions on their flanks, the Russians took the time to occupy Vienna and beat back an attack from the Baltic coast commanded by Heinz Guderian, the Fuhrer's ever-devoted armor enthusiast from the days of Poland and France. On April 16 the Red Army moved on Berlin proper with three separate army groups, the largest of them commanded by the formidable Georgi Zhukov, who also directed the overall assault. The advance broke in almost simultaneously from the north, east, and south as the three Soviet commanders drove their troops, at Stalin's instigation, to see who could enter Berlin first. Pincers meanwhile swept round either edge to close west of the city and prevent its people and defenders from escaping.

Fighting was street to street, often even house to house and room to room, as at Stalingrad. Russian artillery poured thousands of shells into apartment blocks, dwellings, and even back gardens sometimes at point-blank range. In the inner ring near the Brandenburg Gate and the Chancellery, already targeted by the bombers, the heavy guns were merciless. Red soldiers were encouraged to ransack, even given a poundage allotment for loot. They murdered and raped on their own, though with little effective effort to control them.

On April 29 Hitler married his longtime companion, Eva Braun, and dictated his last testament, blaming Germany's defeat on the spinelessness of the German people, on the stupidity and treachery of his generals, and on the Jews, whom he called on German survivors to continue slaughtering. He committed suicide the next day. The Berlin commandant, with no ammunition left, surrendered. On May 1 the Soviet flag floated over the Reichstag, the German parliament building.

At Berlin the Red Army suffered 300,000 casualties and lost hundreds of armored vehicles, many of them to Hitler Youth zealots wielding *panzerfausts,* one-person antitank rocket launchers that were the most effective weapons of their kind in the world, perhaps the closest Hitler would ever come to his vaunted "miracle weapon." The Germans lost nearly as many people as the Red Army, most of them civilians, plus countless others who would bear lasting psychological scars from what historian John Erickson calls the "frenzy and savagery" of this violence. Yet in their day the Germans had destroyed 1,700 Soviet cities and 70,000 villages and had killed 25 million Soviets, the majority of them civilians. For many Russians, Berlin was justice.

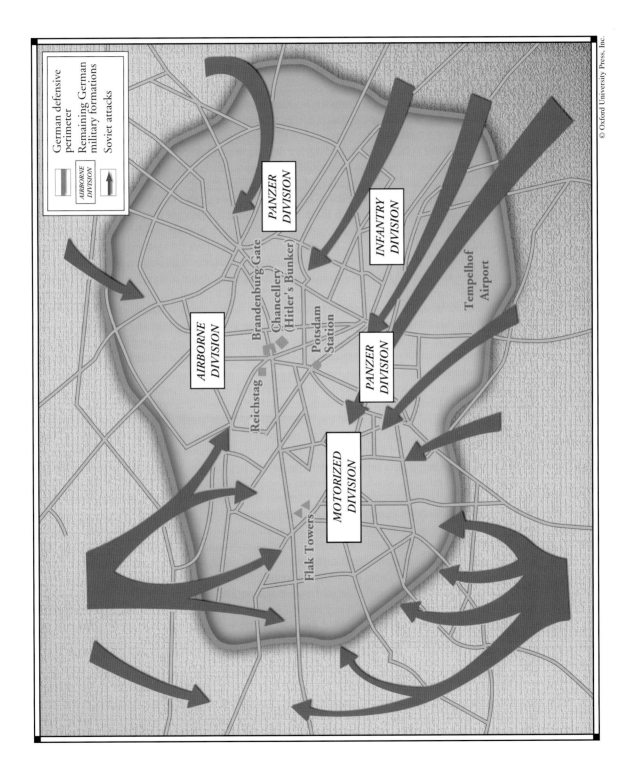

# 31 THE LIBERATION OF THE CAMPS

The Allied armies entering the Third Reich uncovered a vast camp system where Hitler had imprisoned, brutalized, and murdered the subject people of the New Order. The discovery, and liberation, of these camps was one of the transcendent achievements of the soldiers of the Grand Alliance and all humanity.

There were four main types of camp: concentration, labor, extermination, and POW. The Nazis established the first concentration camp for political and other "undesirables" at Dachau in southern Germany in 1933, the year they gained power. Others followed, including the dreaded complex at Buchenwald in the center of the country. By 1938 there were six major camps holding perhaps 50,000 people, but the system accelerated during the war to comprise dozens of camps. At first they held German Marxists, liberals, and other political enemies. During the war there were also various classes of criminals, "shiftless" unemployed, homosexuals, gypsies, Russians, Poles, and others from occupied countries, especially Jews. By 1944 the concentration camps held some 500,000 people, but many more passed through them because of the 50 percent death rate from malnutrition, disease, hard labor, mistreatment, and murder. Though not extermination camps per se, Buchenwald and other big camps had gas chambers and crematoria for systematic murder, mostly of Jews, and "clinics" for grisly live medical experiments, performed mainly on Jews.

There were also some 1,600 labor camps, many attached to larger concentration camps as satellites and others standing alone. In the early years the SS, which ran all the non-POW camps, forced the inmates to work in SS-owned plants and mines, but during the war Krupp and other corporations employed this slave labor. The death rates in some labor camps was as great as in the concentration camps, so as war production picked up, the demand for fresh laborers to replace the old grew exponentially, adding to the frenzied exploitation of the occupied countries. Late in the war the Reich contained 8 million foreign forced laborers.

There were also six immense death camps in Poland designed specifically for mass killing. These usually had labor camps attached to them, but their purpose, in accordance with Hitler's doctrines of German racial supremacy and the need for pure, hardy stock, was systematic, large-scale murder. The Nazis killed more than 5 million Jews, over half the Jewish population of Europe. They killed some in the ghettoes of Eastern Europe, others in mass executions in Russia. Most died in the death camps, including over a million at Auschwitz, the largest, most sinister facility of its kind in history. They also killed hundreds of thousands of gypsies and hundreds of thousands of disabled, mentally ill, and what the SS termed other "defectives," including antiwar "left-wing neurotics." Few who entered the death camps left alive.

There were also extensive POW camps. Here conditions varied. As one index, the death rate for French and other Westerners of "Nordic" or "quasi-Nordic" stock was generally less than 10 percent. But Slavs were considered subhumans. A half-million Soviets were handed over to the SS for immediate killing on racial or political grounds. Millions of others died in captivity.

American and British troops liberated concentration and slave labor camps, most of which were in Germany proper or Austria. They reacted to what they found with disbelief, shock, horror, and disgust. Allied commanders provided food, medicine, and clothing that saved thousands, but the magnitude was overwhelming. Some commanders (Patton was one) allowed their basic anti-Semitism to get in the way of humane treatment of surviving Jews. In some places German civilians, though former enemies, received better treatment than the liberated camp inmates. Red Army soldiers reacted similarly to the death camps, although they found fewer survivors. Stalin, incredibly, sent liberated Soviet POWs to Siberian holding camps on the grounds that they might be secret fascist or Western sympathizers. Everywhere the SS tried but failed to eradicate the signs of what they had done, leaving much evidence for the coming war crimes trials.

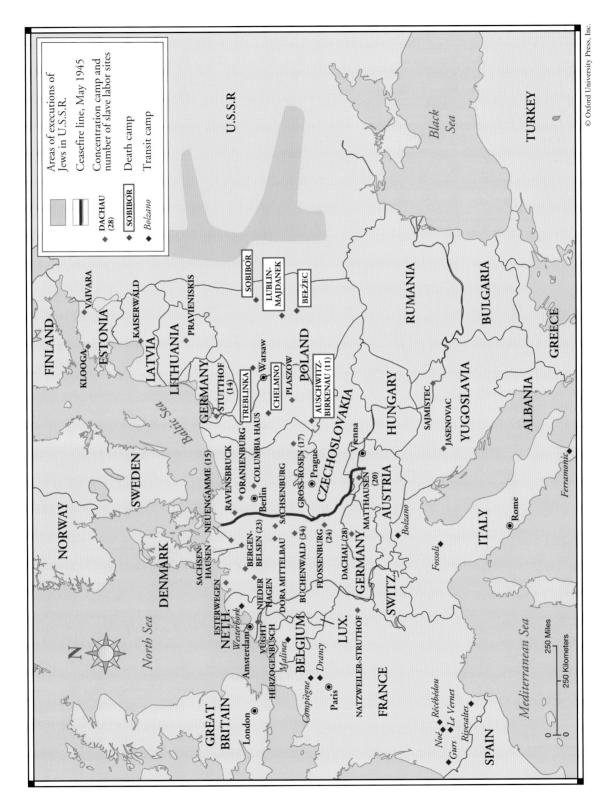

**Legend:**

Areas of executions of Jews in U.S.S.R.

Ceasefire line, May 1945

Concentration camp and number of slave labor sites

DACHAU (28)

◆ Death camp

SOBIBÓR Death camp

*Bolzano* Transit camp

**Countries/Regions:** FINLAND, NORWAY, SWEDEN, U.S.S.R., ESTONIA, LATVIA, LITHUANIA, DENMARK, GERMANY, POLAND, GREAT BRITAIN, NETH., BELGIUM, LUX., FRANCE, SWITZ., AUSTRIA, CZECHOSLOVAKIA, HUNGARY, RUMANIA, YUGOSLAVIA, BULGARIA, ITALY, ALBANIA, GREECE, TURKEY, SPAIN

**Bodies of water:** North Sea, Baltic Sea, Black Sea, Mediterranean Sea

**Camps/Sites:** VAIVARA, KLOOGA, KAISERWALD, PRAVENISKIS, SOBIBÓR, LUBLIN-MAJDANEK, BEŁŻEC, STUTTHOF (14), TREBLINKA, Warsaw, CHELMNO, PLASZOW, AUSCHWITZ-BIRKENAU (11), RAVENSBRUCK, ORANIENBURG, COLUMBIA HAUS, Berlin, SACHSENBURG, GROSS-ROSEN (17), Prague, Vienna, MATTHAUSEN (20), NEUENGAMME (15), SACHSENHAUSEN, BERGEN-BELSEN (23), DORA MITTELBAU, BUCHENWALD (34), FLOSSENBURG (24), DACHAU (28), Bolzano, SAJMISTEC, JASENOVAC, Ferramonic, Rome, Fossoli, ESTERWEGEN, NIEDERHAGEN, VUGHT, Westerbork, Amsterdam, HERZOGENBUSCH, Malines, Drancy, Compiegne, Paris, London, NATZWEILER-STRUTHOF, Noé, Récébédou, Le Vernet, Gurs, Rivesaltes

**Cities:** London, Amsterdam, Paris, Berlin, Prague, Vienna, Warsaw, Rome

N

*North Sea*

250 Miles
250 Kilometers

# 32 OCCUPIED GERMANY

German officers signed unconditional surrender documents at Eisenhower's headquarters in Rheims on May 8, 1945. This ended the European war and fulfilled the Roosevelt-Churchill pledge of total victory. The occupation itself, which Roosevelt believed essential to the destruction of Nazi tyranny and Prussian militarism and the prevention of another war, followed military realities and the prior agreements of the Big Three. The Americans withdrew their forces a little from central Germany to allow the U.S.S.R. to take control of previously agreed-on territory and withdrew from the south to permit France, at de Gaulle's insistence, to play a role in the occupation. France asked for all of Germany west of the Rhine but failed to get it, even though Poland got a chunk of eastern Germany. Berlin, though in the Soviet zone, was internationalized, with four occupation zones (like the partitioning of the country as a whole). Austria, separated again from Germany, followed a similar pattern.

The Allied Powers had two overriding, sometimes contradictory, concerns. They needed to revive the economy of a country where half the buildings were rubble, starvation threatened, millions of workers lay dead on the battlefield, and millions of refugees were streaming in from the east. But they also feared Germany and wanted to render it stable and friendly and not a threat to peace. The Russians insisted, understandably, on reparations and took them by appropriating German factories and raw materials wholesale and breaking up the Prussian landed estates, measures that weakened Germany but made it less self-sufficient. The United States and Britain wanted to dismantle the industrial cartels that had sustained the war—Roosevelt even toyed with "pastoralizing" Germany to pull its teeth—but reversed themselves to facilitate recovery. Occupation economic restrictions made it hard to trade manufactures in one sector for food in another. But deindustrialization and anticartel measures slowed, at least in the Western sectors. Investment and trade grew. East-West tensions drove the Western powers closer, which boosted collaboration, and the U.S. Marshall Plan aid began to flow. By 1950 a German "economic miracle" underpinned the transition to democracy.

A unified German government never emerged. Hence there was no formal peace treaty. Stalin seemed comfortable with a unified parliamentary system as long as he thought the German Communist Party might win elections. When that became unlikely, he constructed a totalitarian People's Republic of Germany, with its capital in Berlin. The Western powers sponsored a Federal Republic of Germany, headquartered in Bonn, with party competition and free labor unions, freedom of religion and the press, and free universities.

The West Germans took easily to democratization. There was a revulsion against nationalism and authoritarianism because of the ruin they had brought to Germany. The ruin in turn engendered a kind of demoralized willingness to adopt democracy without complaint if that was what the victors wanted. It helped that the chief zealots of reaction were mostly dead, that the divide between the Soviets and the West looked permanent, and that the United States alone had nuclear weapons. Without advocates, unity, and miracle weapons, a resurgent Germany was unthinkable. In 1919 the French and others wanted Germany militarily weak and politically divided. In 1945 that's what they got, though not quite in the way they wished.

The occupying Powers allowed former Nazis to hold administrative positions because the Nazi Party had been so large and pervasive that there was hardly anyone else to run things. But they tried to de-Nazify the country by indicting German war leaders before an International Military Tribunal in Nuremberg. Most were convicted of crimes against humanity, peace, and acceptable military conduct. Each Western power held trials in its own sector, as did the Federal Republic, which brought people to the bar of justice for decades, though with fewer convictions and lighter sentences as time passed. The Federal Republic also acknowledged German culpability in the Holocaust and paid reparations, an acceptance of national responsibility for past evil that is almost unique in history.

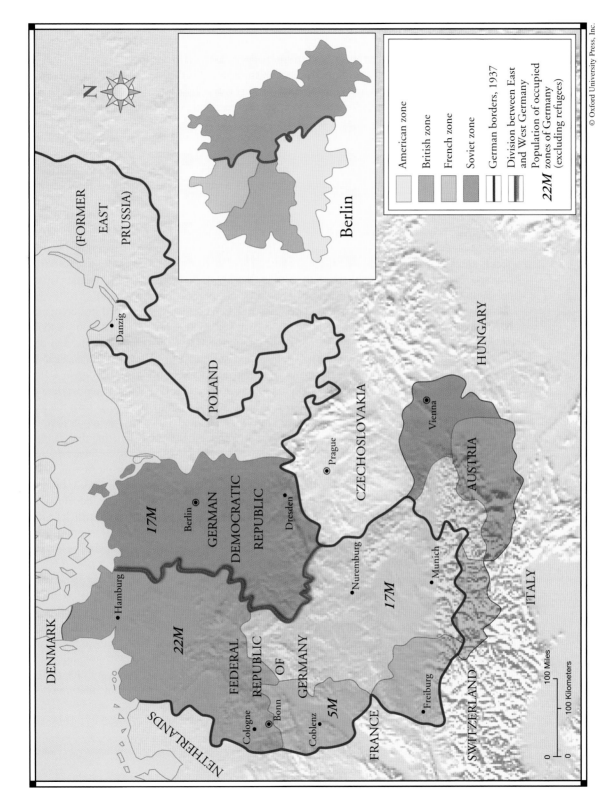

N

**Legend:**
- American zone
- British zone
- French zone
- Soviet zone
- German borders, 1937
- Division between East and West Germany
- 22M Population of occupied zones of Germany (excluding refugees)

Berlin

DENMARK

(FORMER EAST PRUSSIA)

• Danzig

POLAND

NETHERLANDS

• Hamburg

17M

Berlin ◉

GERMAN DEMOCRATIC REPUBLIC

• Dresden

CZECHOSLOVAKIA

◉ Prague

HUNGARY

Vienna ◉

AUSTRIA

22M

FEDERAL REPUBLIC OF GERMANY

Cologne •
◉ Bonn
Coblenz •

5M

• Nuremburg

17M

• Munich

FRANCE

• Freiburg

SWITZERLAND

ITALY

0    100 Miles
0    100 Kilometers

# 33 POSTWAR EUROPE

Except for boundary adjustments in Eastern Europe, the map of Europe in the late 1940s looked like 1919: same countries and mostly the same frontiers. But the map was misleading. Four developments of enormous importance were transforming the continent.

Development one was the Cold War, which extended the German-Austrian pattern of a closed Soviet zone in the east and democratic capitalist zones in the west. By 1948 East Germany, Poland, Czechoslovakia, Hungary, Rumania, and Bulgaria as well as the Baltic states were satellites of the U.S.S.R., which exploited their economies and controlled their governments. But there were variations. Communist Yugoslavia, where partisans rather than the Red Army had defeated the Germans, soon asserted its independence. Communist Albania, in a curious twist, followed the People's Republic of China's lead rather than Moscow's.

Western Europe, by contrast, developed strong democratic capitalist systems, with competing political parties, private property, independent media and universities, and free trade unions. There were bumps on the road to democratization, including a civil war in Greece and enduring dictatorships in Portugal and Spain. But after fascism and Nazism, there was a broad commitment to free institutions, even a willingness to defend them militarily through the North Atlantic Treaty Organization (NATO), an alliance created in 1949 with U.S. sponsorship and support.

Development two was the presence and power of the United States, which had lost comparatively few lives and experienced little fighting on its own soil. With a revitalized economy and an expanded military, the United States was by default one of the world's two superpowers, and this time the Americans stayed the course. They joined and sustained the United Nations, dear to Roosevelt's heart, and a host of other international organizations; kept troops in Europe to watch first the Germans and then the Russians; supplied billions of Marshall Plan dollars; and worked to maintain cordial relations even with, for example, France, which eventually built its own nuclear arsenal and withdrew from active participation in NATO. The United States was an unprecedented player in postwar European affairs, reversing age-old diplomatic habits and signaling that Europe was no longer the world's sole power center.

Development three was the collapse of the colonial empires. British India went first in 1947; other British colonies followed, including all the African possessions depicted in Map 2. France, too, relinquished its colonies, though with more bloodshed, especially in Algeria and Indochina. In the 1950s Charles de Gaulle became president of France to resolve the Algerian crisis, which he did by granting the Algerians their independence—an irony given his wartime reliance on support from the colonies for Free France. Decolonization marked the end of free access to imperial resources and markets and the reorientation of the West European economic order.

Development four was perhaps the most profound. This had two parts. First, each democratic country in Western Europe rewarded its people for their wartime sacrifice and suffering by establishing welfare states with high rates of taxation and high social benefits, including medical care, university education, unemployment and old age insurance, and housing subsidies. Second, statesmen in Germany and France labored to forge a lasting peace by tying the economies of these two ancient adversaries together. They created in succession the Coal and Steel Community, the Common Market, and the European Union, each with Franco-German collaboration at its heart. The welfare states damped down the continent's explosive political extremism; economic unity moderated its impulse to war. Western Europe became a safer, freer place.

### Legend

- U.S.S.R. in 1938
- Added to U.S.S.R., 1939-1945
- Soviet satellites
- Communist ally of China after 1949
- Communist, non-satellite
- Military dictatorship
- Parliamentary democracy

**N**

U.S.S.R

Moscow

FINLAND

ESTONIA

LATVIA

LITHUANIA

NORWAY

Oslo

SWEDEN

Baltic Sea

Danzig

Warsaw

POLAND

Berlin

GERMAN DEM. REPUBLIC

CZECHOSLOVAKIA

HUNGARY

ROMANIA

BULGARIA

Black Sea

DENMARK

North Sea

NETH.

BELGIUM

LUX.

Bonn

GERMAN FEDERAL REPUBLIC

SWITZ.

Vienna

AUSTRIA

YUGOSLAVIA

Belgrade

ALBANIA

GREECE

Athens

TURKEY

Cyprus

SYRIA

Crete

IRELAND

GREAT BRITAIN

London

Paris

FRANCE

ITALY

Rome

Corsica

Sardinia

Mediterranean Sea

Sicily

ATLANTIC OCEAN

PORTUGAL

SPAIN

Madrid

ALGERIA (Fr.)

MOROCCO

TUNISIA

0        500 Miles

0        500 Kilometers

# 34 ASIA IN THE EARLY 20<sup>TH</sup> CENTURY

The background to World War Two in Asia and the Pacific was colonialism and colonial ambition. As was the case in Africa, the Western Powers ruled virtually the entire Asian region from the western edge of India to the main Pacific island groups, including the American protectorate of Hawaii, three thousand miles east of the Marianas.

The most imposing presence was Great Britain. The "jewel of the crown" was India, first conquered, controlled, and exploited by the private East India Company and ruled directly by the British government through an appointed viceroy from the mid-19<sup>th</sup> century. The British built railroads; expanded the production of cotton, opium, and other cash crops; and turned the subcontinent into a protected market closed to all but British investment and trade. The British dealt similarly with Ceylon, at India's southern tip, and (by the late 19<sup>th</sup> century) with Burma, governed as an Indian province.

Next to fall under the sway of the eastward-moving British was the Malayan peninsula with its magnificent harbor, Singapore, together providing not only raw materials but control of a key trade route. Beyond French Indo-China were Hong Kong and various "treaty ports" on the China coast as well as immense transportation investments in the Chinese interior. British troops and warships, supported by "native" Indian military units, maintained control of this vast and (save for China) closed system. Far to the south were the British dominions of Australia and New Zealand, peopled and governed by British descendants fiercely committed to the United Kingdom, to a "whites-only" immigration policy, and to the British system of imperial trade preferences.

France possessed the rubber-producing region of Indo-China and, like Britain, had significant commercial and investment interests in China. The Netherlands controlled the oil-rich East Indies lying between Malaya and Australia. The United States governed the Philippines, won from Spain in 1898 and valuable chiefly as a way station for the China trade. To the north were Japan, a newcomer to Asian conquest (like the United States) but with a hold by now over Korea and the big island of Formosa off the South China coast, and Russia, not yet a major colonial force but with a long-standing stake in Mongolia, investments in China, a warm-water port at Vladivostok, and an inclination to exert its interests if possible. The toppling of the tsar in 1917 damaged these ambitions but did not extinguish them. Germany would lose its modest possessions—island groups in the western Pacific and lucrative investments in China below Peking, including breweries at Tsingtao—at the Versailles Conference of 1919.

The Great Powers were in Asia almost solely for profit. Britain got gold, copper, grain, dairy products, wool, and meat from Australia and New Zealand; cotton, rice, tea, timber, and cocoa from India; spices, tin, and rubber from other colonies; and silk and rice from its activities in China. Other European powers got not only rubber and tin but oil, fruit, coffee, tobacco, and palm products. They also got high returns on shipping, mining, and railroad investments, which by 1914 amounted to some $5 billion, and they got such important captive markets for their manufactured products that significant sectors of the European economies were oriented to "the Orient." There was clearly some reason to fight to maintain these valuable Asian possessions, should it come to that. As it turned out, the United States and Japan, the two powers with perhaps the smallest economic stake in the region as of 1914, would end up doing most of the fighting in World War Two.

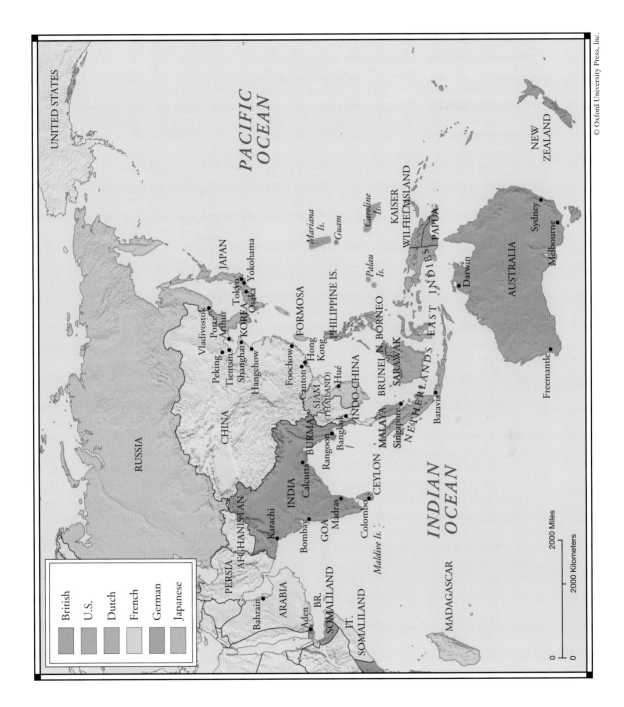

UNITED STATES

PACIFIC
OCEAN

RUSSIA

CHINA

JAPAN
Tokyo
Yokohama
Osaka
KOREA
Port
Arthur
Vladivostok
Peking
Tientsin
Shanghai
Hangchow
Foochow
FORMOSA
Canton
Hong
Kong
Hué
SIAM
(THAILAND)
Bangkok
BURMA
Rangoon
INDO-CHINA
PHILIPPINE IS.

Mariana
Is.
Guam

Caroline
Is.

Palau
Is.

KAISER
WILHELMSLAND
PAPUA
EAST INDIES

BRUNEI
N. BORNEO
SARAWAK
MALAYA
Singapore
NETHERLANDS
Batavia

Darwin

AUSTRALIA

Sydney
Melbourne

Freemantle

NEW
ZEALAND

AFGHANISTAN
INDIA
Karachi
Bombay
GOA
Madras
Calcutta
CEYLON
Colombo
Maldive Is.

INDIAN
OCEAN

PERSIA
ARABIA
Bahrain
Aden
BR.
SOMALILAND
FT.
SOMALILAND
IT.
SOMALILAND

MADAGASCAR

British
U.S.
Dutch
French
German
Japanese

2000 Miles
2000 Kilometers
0
0

© Oxford University Press, Inc.

73

# 35 | CHINA IN THE EARLY 20<sup>TH</sup> CENTURY

Europe's growing control over Asia came partly at the expense of Imperial China, long the cultural and economic suzerain of the region but increasingly weak, even if nominally independent. China's independence was due mainly to its vast size and population, extensive cultural influence, generations of more or less stable agricultural prosperity under the Ch'ing (or Manchu) dynasty, and the remarkable unity provided by an educated Confucian civil service. Weakness, however, emerged in the 19<sup>th</sup> century. Drought, floods, and an expanding population produced rural misery and widespread unrest, as evidenced in the Tai-ping Rebellion in central China, which lasted 15 years and took over 20 million lives before succumbing to imperial government forces backed by foreign troops.

The Manchus were also not able to keep the British from selling opium (a known debilitating drug) along the Yangtze River; to keep the European Powers from establishing treaty ports on the coast, with special privileges for foreign traders; or to keep competitors from taking territory. The British took Hong Kong, and Russia took territory in the northeast and northwest. Germany extracted a concession around Shantung. France assumed control of Indochina, a former tributary, while Japan, after winning the Sino-Japanese War of 1894–1895, took Formosa and Korea.

The Great Powers meanwhile built railroads into the Chinese interior and developed economic "spheres of influence" that brought Chinese wealth—and Chinese destiny—increasingly into the hands of foreign investors. The Manchu dynasty, now too weak to collect the taxes required to run the bureaucracy or the military, covered its expenses by borrowing at hefty rates from the foreigners, who took over the Chinese customhouses to ensure that the loans would be repaid. By 1900 Chinese cities had foreign enclaves with their own police, courts, commercial institutions, and laws; Christian missionaries swarmed everywhere. In much of the country, Manchu authority no longer held sway.

In 1900 rebel peasants and workers around Peking rose up against the landlords and the shaky Manchu throne in the Boxer Rebellion. The dynasty survived only by shifting attention to the "foreign devils." The Boxers obligingly besieged the foreign legations, destroyed foreign property, and murdered missionaries and others until an international force, dominated by Japanese but including American troops from the new U.S. colony in the Philippines, marched into Peking, killed thousands of rebels, and forced the government at gunpoint to agree to ruinous reparations for the Boxer destruction. Without power or prestige and unable to modernize its economy, its politics, or its military, the Manchu dynasty collapsed in 1911.

The independence of China at the dawn of the 20<sup>th</sup> century was largely illusory, while China's weakness, particularly in modern industry and military power, was real. The country lay wounded and seemingly helpless before its adversaries, especially its cousins to the east, the Japanese, who were the most ambitious and aggressive of them all. China's weakness, as it turned out, was only partial—paralysis rather than death—as a colonizing Japan would discover. China's weakness helped precipitate World War Two; China's resistance helped shape it. Nevertheless, it would take a century and rivers of blood for the Chinese Dragon to rise again.

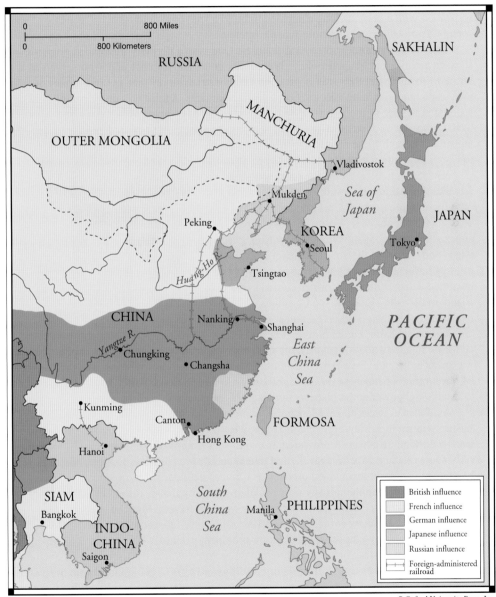

Japan in the 19th century was feudal, agrarian, and isolated, possessing neither the means nor the will to participate in the subjugation of China. But the Japanese could see what was happening to the Chinese and what, by extension, might happen to them, a point driven home when the United States and Britain forced them to sign trade agreements similar to those forced on China. They responded with a decades-long campaign to build a "national defense state" capable of warding off foreign depredation and asserting Japan's interests.

This transformation had several features. One was a divinely descended emperor, who transcended politics but shaped policy through his court and cabinet and who served as a focus of absolute loyalty. Another was a program of industrialization that poured money into railroads, heavy machinery, mining, electric power, and armaments. A third was universal military service and training in the use of modern weapons. The army and navy held cabinet posts and reported directly to the emperor. A system of universal schooling ensured literacy and promoted devotion to the emperor. Through these means, Japan would become an economic and military power impervious to China-like humiliations.

Since colonialism seemed coterminous with power in the 19th century—and since Japan was remarkably resource-poor—the campaign inevitably developed expansionist goals. These centered initially on Korea, which China and Russia also coveted. Japan's victory over China in the war of 1894–1895, fought over Korea, brought Japan control of Formosa and most of Korea (formally annexed in 1910). Japan's victory over Russia in the war of 1904–1905 brought southern Sakhalin Island and control of the South Manchurian Railway, which became a vehicle for major investments in Manchuria and a reason to deploy troops in the area. The Versailles peace settlements of 1919 rewarded Japan with both former German interests on the Shantung Peninsula and three Pacific island groups (the Marianas, the Carolines, and the Marshalls), though these were League of Nation mandates rather than outright colonies, which irritated Tokyo.

Korea, Sakhalin, the Pacific islands, and Formosa were all fairly straightforward security concerns. In Shantung and Manchuria, the motives were mainly economic: the exploitation of Chinese weakness in the old Great Powers tradition. Manchuria, rich in soybeans, iron ore, and coal, was in fact becoming for Japanese policy makers what India and South Africa had been for Britain—a key to wealth and power and a place to settle surplus population.

As Japan's interests in Manchuria increased, so did its military commitment. The large Japanese army in Kwantung, stationed just west of Korea to police the region, became in fact a quasi-autonomous player. It pressured Tokyo to seek complete domination of Manchuria, and possibly Mongolia and Siberia as well, and maneuvered to establish a puppet Chinese government in Manchuria, a project that gained urgency as Chinese nationalist fervor spread northward. In 1931 a bomb exploded along the railway near Mukden. Japanese troops rushed in and within months controlled the whole of Manchuria. Within two years a former Manchu emperor was the head of "Manchukuo"; Japanese officials, however, ran every government agency. Manchukuo then annexed, for security purposes, the abutting province of Jehol.

Chinese nationalists bitterly protested these seizures, which led to fighting in Shanghai in 1932 and constant low-level conflict that finally boiled over in 1937, prompting Japan to send troops into central China. Chiang Kai-shek's army fought back, blowing the Yellow River dikes, for example, to slow the advancing Japanese; fighting hard in Shanghai; and withdrawing from the capital, Nanking, to Chungking in the interior. The Japanese never subdued Chungking; they did, however, subdue Nanking, killing tens of thousands of civilians in the notorious "Rape of Nanking" during which Japanese soldiers beheaded, disemboweled, and raped Chinese in a frenzy of bloody violence.

By 1939 Japan, weak and defenseless in 1870, controlled enough land and population to make it one of the world's foremost imperial powers. That, it turned out, was not enough.

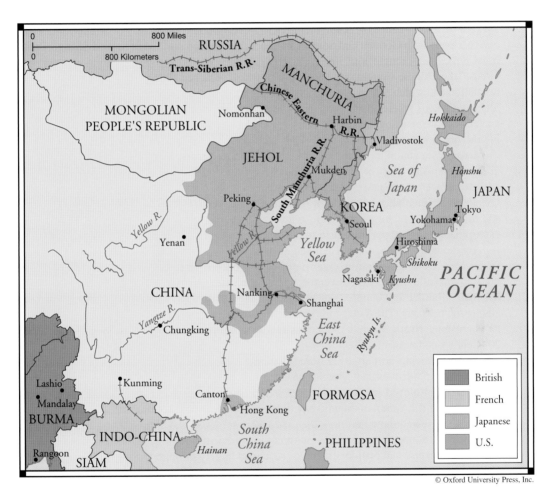

RUSSIA

Trans-Siberian R.R.

MONGOLIAN
PEOPLE'S REPUBLIC

MANCHURIA

Chinese Eastern R.R.

Nomonhan

Harbin

Hokkaido

JEHOL

South Manchuria R.R.

Vladivostok

Mukden

Sea of
Japan

Honshu

Peking

KOREA

Seoul

JAPAN

Tokyo

Yellow R.

Yokohama

Yenan

Hiroshima

Yellow
Sea

Shikoku

CHINA

Nanking

Nagasaki

Kyushu

PACIFIC
OCEAN

Yangtze R.

Shanghai

Chungking

East
China
Sea

Ryukyu Is.

Kunming

Canton

FORMOSA

British

French

Lashio

Hong Kong

Japanese

Mandalay

U.S.

BURMA

INDO-CHINA

South
China
Sea

PHILIPPINES

Rangoon

SIAM

Hainan

0        800 Miles
0        800 Kilometers

© Oxford University Press, Inc.

77

# 37 CHINA DIVIDED—THE LONG MARCH

Unlike Japan, Imperial China did not embark on a crash program to modernize its economy and military. Instead, battered by domestic unrest and Western economic penetration, the Manchu dynasty grew steadily weaker until its replacement in 1911 by a republican government dedicated to representative democracy and economic justice. But national unity proved elusive, and the country soon degenerated into "warlordism," with different provinces controlled by primitively armed troops loyal to a local governor or general. China seethed with frustrated nationalism and with hostility toward the "foreign devils" but was unable to muster enough force to redress its grievances.

This started to change in the 1920s when a young general, Chiang Kai-shek, took over a nationalist political party called the Kuomintang (KMT), consolidated his power in South China, strengthened his army with German and Soviet assistance, and moved northward toward Shanghai and central China. This brought him into conflict with other warlords and, more importantly, with the "Reds," the Chinese Community Party (CCP), which preached Chinese liberation through socialist revolution and which had strong support from China's intelligentsia and blue-collar workers. When Shanghai's Reds greeted the approach of Chiang's army with a massive general strike, he turned on and crushed them, using the help of Chinese merchants and the foreign business community, including the Japanese.

Faced with annihilation, the Communists abandoned their urban working-class base, relocated in the countryside west of Shanghai, and reconfigured both their ideology and their movement, against the wishes of Russia, to represent the interests of poor peasants rather than poor workers, a novelty in the revolutionary world of that era. Chiang, recognizing this as a threat to Chinese unity and his own political base among the gentry and merchants, conducted a series of ruthless "bandit extermination campaigns" designed to destroy this new peasant-based Communist insurgency.

By the mid-1930s Chiang's campaigns were succeeding. The Communists, under their young leader Mao Tse-tung, therefore determined to flee once again. Thus ensued the "Long March" of the Red guerrilla armies across central China to a safe haven in Shensi Province, just below the Mongolian border and hundreds of miles from the Sea of Japan, where they could build support among the peasants. The 6,000-mile march, involving confrontations with KMT forces, local warlords, rushing rivers, rugged mountains, and the elements, became a legend in the annals of 20th-century communism.

Chiang, having scattered his domestic foes, took control of the Nationalist government in Nanking and plotted further assaults on the Communists. When Japan consolidated its hold on Manchuria and moved into central China in the late 1930s, Chiang and Mao declared a truce in order to resist the common enemy, but there was no real collaboration or joint military strategy because each feared the other more than the Japanese. Japan ended up fighting two foes in China: in the north, Communist guerrillas employing low-grade hit-and-run sabotage tactics; in the south, ill-trained conventional Nationalist forces sustained largely through U.S. Lend-Lease support. The Chinese refusal to surrender forced Japan to keep 2 million soldiers in China and expend resources there that it could not afford. But neither the KMT nor the CCP really wanted to fight pitched battles. Each understood that a U.S. victory would trigger a showdown for control of China; it would be far better to avoid Japanese attacks and reprisals and build strength for the looming civil war.

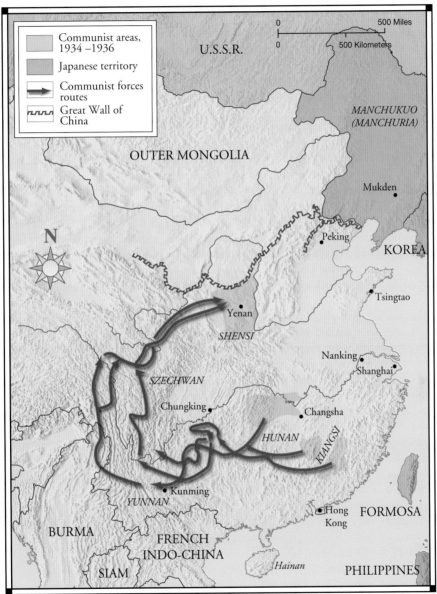

# 38    Pearl Harbor

Japan's conquests had brought few immediate benefits by 1941, particularly in the area of key resources such as oil and rubber that the Japanese military, like its counterparts everywhere, had to have. China not only had little oil but was becoming a quagmire for the Japanese, who were unable to subdue either the Nationalists or the Communists and who risked expending more resources there than they could extract. Things would get worse if Roosevelt sent military aid to Chungking, as seemed likely. By 1941 Japanese naval chiefs openly derided the army's promise to pacify China and urged the government instead to authorize a move south into British Malaya, which had rubber, and the Netherlands East Indies, which had oil. With Hitler battering the colonial powers in Europe, the time seemed ripe. The emperor and his advisors agreed and so, finally, did the army. Japan arranged with Vichy France to acquire bases in Indochina for the southern advance.

The risk in this strategy was obvious. The main objective was the Indies, from which oil would be transported to Japan. But the Philippines, a U.S. colony, were directly astride the shipping lanes. If the Americans entered the war on the Allied side, this would constitute an intolerable threat to the oil supplies. Taking the Philippines would eliminate this threat, but it would also trigger U.S. retaliation, and not even Admiral Yamamoto Isoroku, the brilliant architect of the southern strategy, thought Japan could defeat the United States, the world's greatest industrial power, in an all-out conflict.

Ordered to develop a plan of attack, Yamamoto nevertheless went all out. He argued that if the Japanese invaded Malaya and the Indies, they had to invade the Philippines, too, to prevent future trouble. But because the United States was certain to retaliate, Japan—and here was Yamamoto's most explosive point—should destroy the U.S. Pacific fleet at Pearl Harbor in the Hawaiian Islands before it could move into the western Pacific. This would give Japan time to build a strong defensive perimeter and perhaps persuade the Americans, preoccupied with Europe, to accept a truce.

Neither side wanted war right away: Roosevelt thought war would make the fight against Germany harder; Tokyo thought war might threaten its new empire. Negotiations therefore continued between Tokyo and Washington into late 1941. Japan argued that the Americans should sell them oil and metals and stop helping Chiang Kai-shek. The United States wanted the Japanese to withdraw from their alliance with Germany and remove their troops from Indochina and China. The talks finally came to nothing because the Japanese were committed to their southern strategy and the Americans would not abandon Chiang or Britain.

U.S. intelligence indicated that a strike was likely sometime around December 7, but probably against the Philippines, not Hawaii. The Japanese strike force of 6 carriers, with 400 planes plus battleships, cruisers, and destroyers, maintained strict radio silence, a remarkable exercise in self-discipline over so long an approach. December 7 was a Sunday, when the Americans were sleeping off Saturday night escapades and were at half-crew. Surprise was therefore total. At a cost of 29 planes and less than 70 dead, the Japanese sank or damaged 8 battleships and 5 destroyers, destroyed or damaged 250 planes, killed 2,300 Americans, and wounded 1,100. The strike force commanders withdrew well satisfied.

They should not have been. The damage was heavy but repairable and spared the most vital warships and installations. The American carriers were away on ferry duty and escaped attack, and the sprawling Pearl Harbor oil storage tanks survived intact. Many Americans died, but not enough to affect future operations. All but two of the battleships were repaired and they fought again. The strike, moreover, had an unforeseen but profound consequence: It enraged the American public, who erupted in a fury of revenge, racism, and resolve. However logical it might have seemed to Yamamoto, the raid on Pearl Harbor would make the Pacific war a fight to the death.

## A. Japanese Approach

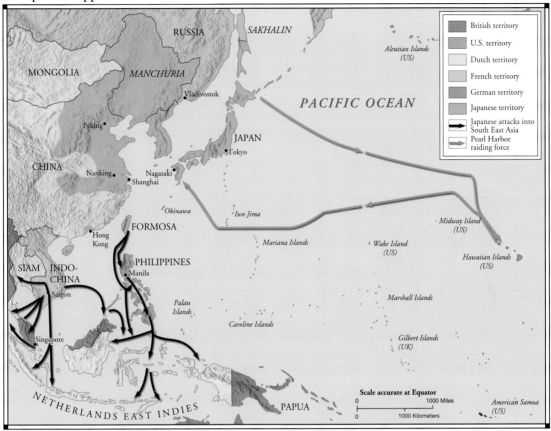

**British territory**
**U.S. territory**
**Dutch territory**
**French territory**
**German territory**
**Japanese territory**
Japanese attacks into South East Asia
Pearl Harbor raiding force

RUSSIA
SAKHALIN
MONGOLIA
MANCHURIA
Vladivostok
PACIFIC OCEAN
Aleutian Islands (US)
Peking
JAPAN
Tokyo
CHINA
Nanking
Nagasaki
Shanghai
Okinawa
Iwo Jima
Midway Island (US)
FORMOSA
Mariana Islands
Wake Island (US)
Hong Kong
Hawaiian Islands (US)
PHILIPPINES
Manila
SIAM
INDO-CHINA
Saigon
Palau Islands
Marshall Islands
Caroline Islands
Singapore
Gilbert Islands (UK)
NETHERLANDS EAST INDIES
PAPUA
American Samoa (US)

**Scale accurate at Equator**
0    1000 Miles
0    1000 Kilometers

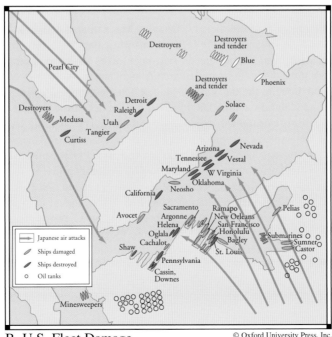

Japanese air attacks
Ships damaged
Ships destroyed
Oil tanks

Pearl City
Destroyers
Destroyers and tender
Blue
Destroyers and tender
Phoenix
Destroyers
Medusa
Detroit
Raleigh
Solace
Utah
Tangier
Curtiss
Arizona
Nevada
Tennessee
Vestal
Maryland
W Virginia
Oklahoma
California
Neosho
Sacramento
Ramapo
Pelias
Avocet
Argonne
New Orleans
Helena
San Francisco
Oglala
Honolulu
Submarines
Cachalot
Bagley
Sumner
Shaw
St. Louis
Castor
Pennsylvania
Cassin, Downes
Minesweepers

**B. U.S. Fleet Damage**

© Oxford University Press, Inc.

81

# 39 THE CONQUEST OF SOUTHEAST ASIA

Simultaneous with its attack on Pearl Harbor, Japan attacked Hong Kong, Malaya, and the Philippines. The small British Hong Kong garrison, with no air cover and few defenses, held out until Christmas Day and might have lasted longer except that enlisted men were not allowed into the Officers Club, which would have provided good cover.

Malaya, where the British had 80,000 mixed Commonwealth troops and 150 fighter planes, promised to be different, particularly since Britain had fortified and upgunned the great harbor on Singapore Island, the "Rock of the Pacific," and now sent the capital ships *Repulse* and *Prince of Wales* as reinforcements.

The results were no better. Japanese planes from Indochina sank both big ships on December 10, and the British diluted their air cover by scattering their planes on isolated airstrips that the advancing Japanese systematically overran. The best British, Australian, and Indian troops were in North Africa; those in Malaya were ill-trained and ill-equipped and were without tanks. Intelligence was poor because the British, as colonialists, would not rely on the local Malay natives, many of whom welcomed (at least initially) the Japanese as fellow Asians. The huge harbor guns could not be used for inland defense.

The Japanese, by contrast, were well prepared. Crack troops numbering perhaps 60,000 landed just above the Thai-Malaya frontier and moved quickly south along both coasts. They traveled lightly compared to the heavy-laden British, outflanking roadblocks using jungle marches or traveling by water in rubber boats, and they used bicycles to hasten their advances. They had 200 light tanks, 500 planes, and a superb commander, Yamashita Tomoyuki, known hereafter (with reason) as "the Tiger of Malaya." By mid-January the Japanese had taken Kuala Lumpur and had driven to Lahore, across from Singapore, which their bombers pounded daily. In early February the Japanese landed three divisions in northern Singapore. One week later the British, having evacuated all RAF and other key personnel, surrendered. Japan sustained 10,000 total casualties in Malaya, but they killed 9,000 British Commonwealth soldiers, took 130,000 prisoners (the greatest capitulation in British military history), and executed 30,000 Singapore Chinese, mostly for racial and political reasons.

In the Philippines, where General Douglas MacArthur commanded 120,000 mostly Filipino troops, air attacks destroyed half the U.S. aircraft while they were still on the ground, even after the news arrived about Pearl Harbor. Japanese ground forces landed at several points on Luzon, the big island that anchored the northern end of archipelago, and in two weeks swept the opposing Filipino units aside and drove to the outskirts of Manila. On December 27, MacArthur declared Manila an "open city" and withdrew with 50,000 men to the jungles of the Bataan Peninsula. His own headquarters were on rocky little Corregidor in Manila Bay. The "battling bastards of Bataan" held off the Japanese until April; Corregidor held till May. Thousands of American and Filipino prisoners perished in the subsequent "Bataan Death March" to a POW camp. MacArthur, on Roosevelt's orders, left Corregidor for Australia to rake together another army.

The Japanese also advanced westward to secure Thailand and Burma, thereby establishing a wall against possible British retaliation from India. The Japanese swarmed into the Dutch East Indies too, shattering a multinational naval force in the Java Sea and settling into occupation, again with the local population's initial support because they were Asians.

By spring 1942 Imperial Japan stood as the second-largest colonial power on earth. Though Churchill never admitted it, the fall of Singapore marked the end of the long reign of the first colonial power, Britain. The Japanese empire now seemed to contain enough resources to have staying power, should there be time to develop them. In 1942 people said that about Germany, too.

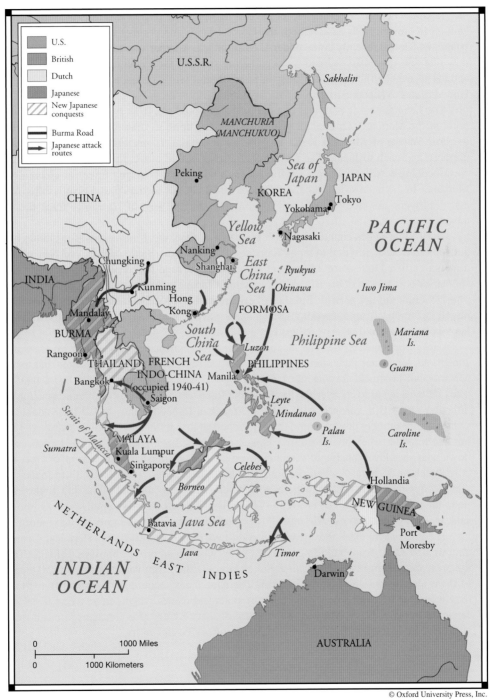

Legend:
- U.S.
- British
- Dutch
- Japanese
- New Japanese conquests
- Burma Road
- Japanese attack routes

U.S.S.R.

Sakhalin

MANCHURIA (MANCHUKUO)

Peking

CHINA

Sea of Japan

JAPAN

KOREA

Tokyo

Yokohama

Nagasaki

Yellow Sea

Nanking

Shanghai

East China Sea

Ryukyus

Okinawa

PACIFIC OCEAN

Iwo Jima

Chungking

Kunming

Hong Kong

FORMOSA

Mariana Is.

INDIA

Mandalay

BURMA

South China Sea

Luzon

Philippine Sea

Guam

Rangoon

THAILAND   FRENCH INDO-CHINA (occupied 1940-41)

Bangkok

Saigon

Manila

PHILIPPINES

Leyte

Mindanao

Palau Is.

Caroline Is.

Strait of Malacca

MALAYA

Kuala Lumpur

Singapore

Celebes

Sumatra

Borneo

Batavia   Java Sea

Hollandia

NEW GUINEA

Port Moresby

NETHERLANDS EAST INDIES

Java

Timor

Darwin

INDIAN OCEAN

AUSTRALIA

0   1000 Miles

0   1000 Kilometers

© Oxford University Press, Inc.

# 40 | THE BATTLE OF MIDWAY

Tokyo undertook its campaign against Midway Island, a U.S. possession just beyond the Japanese defensive perimeter, for several reasons. One reason was to extend the perimeter far enough to prevent raids against both the Home Islands and perimeter strong points such as Wake Island, which had recently come under U.S. air attack. Another was to establish a base near Hawaii now that the Americans seemed to be gathering strength for a counterpunch. Lastly, the Japanese wanted to engage the American fleet in strength and win a climactic battle that might force the United States to accept a truce.

The Japanese battle plan was complex. Forces would sail from two points in Japan and a third point in the Marianas. One major group would head north to draw off the U.S. fleet and occupy the little islands of Attu and Kiska in America's Aleutian Islands, thereby sealing off a possible northern approach to Japan. The main Imperial fleet would move directly toward Midway, on the way shedding a screening force for the Aleutian feint and a covering force for elements from the Marianas. In the main strike force, Japan deployed 4 aircraft carriers plus 11 battleships, 69 cruisers and destroyers, assorted tankers, and a submarine cordon west of Hawaii to track the American advance.

The United States countered with 3 big carriers. One, the *Yorktown*, was available because of a remarkable crash program to repair damage sustained at the Battle of the Coral Sea, off Australia, a month earlier. There were 23 cruisers and destroyers, land-based planes on Midway, and a thin submarine cordon east of the island—no match for Japanese firepower if U.S. aircraft, outnumbered 3 to 2 overall, did not prevail. But the Americans had a hidden advantage: They knew the attack's target and timing from decrypting the Japanese naval code. They therefore refused the feint and kept their carriers and other warships close to Midway.

Luck, too, played a role. The Japanese main force launched strikes against Midway at dawn on June 4. An hour later they were sighted by U.S. carrier planes. Two hours after that, planes from Midway Island struck, forcing the Japanese into evasive maneuvers that delayed their advance. They delayed again to recover the earlier strike force against Midway and then turned north in the direction of the U.S. carriers. At this point American torpedo planes began their attack. Japanese fighter planes quickly dropped onto the 41 lumbering low-flying aircraft and destroyed 35 of them; not one torpedo struck home. But the Japanese fighters, having fought off the torpedo runs, were down near ship level, unable to detect or ward off U.S. carrier-based dive bombers that unexpectedly struck an hour later when the Japanese flight decks were crowded with ordnance and fuel. American bombs damaged 3 Japanese carriers, all scuttled by the end of the day. In the early afternoon the remaining Imperial carrier, the *Hiryu,* launched an air strike against the *Yorktown,* which sank two days later. But the *Hiryu* itself soon suffered a fatal hit and sank the next morning.

The great naval clash the Japanese sought thus turned against them. They lost 4 carriers, 322 aircraft, and 3,000 dead, including valuable pilots who would prove almost as difficult to replace as the great ships themselves. The United States lost only the *Yorktown,* 1 destroyer, 150 planes (many of them already obsolete), and 360 dead. The Americans secured the approaches to Hawaii, and they won time to await a new generation of ships and planes scheduled to arrive in 1943. For the Japanese Imperial Navy, Midway was the equivalent of Kursk for Germany, a clash that left it a still-formidable foe but that forever crippled its offensive capability.

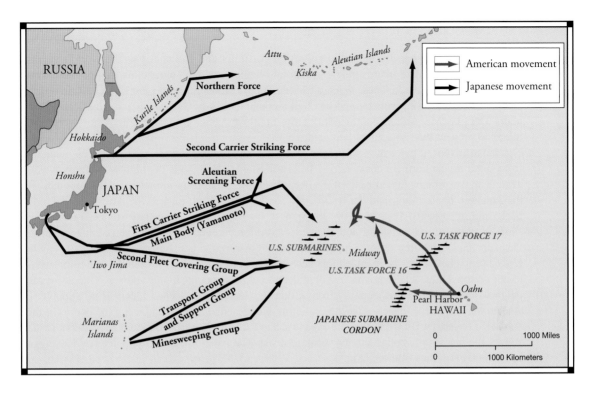

RUSSIA

Attu

Aleutian Islands

Kiska

Kurile Islands

**Northern Force**

Hokkaido

**Second Carrier Striking Force**

Honshu

JAPAN

Tokyo

**Aleutian Screening Force**

*First Carrier Striking Force*

*Main Body (Yamamoto)*

*Second Fleet Covering Group*

U.S. SUBMARINES

Midway

U.S. TASK FORCE 17

U.S. TASK FORCE 16

*Transport Group and Support Group*

*Minesweeping Group*

Oahu

Pearl Harbor

HAWAII

JAPANESE SUBMARINE CORDON

Iwo Jima

Marianas Islands

→ American movement

→ Japanese movement

| 0 | 1000 Miles |
| 0 | 1000 Kilometers |

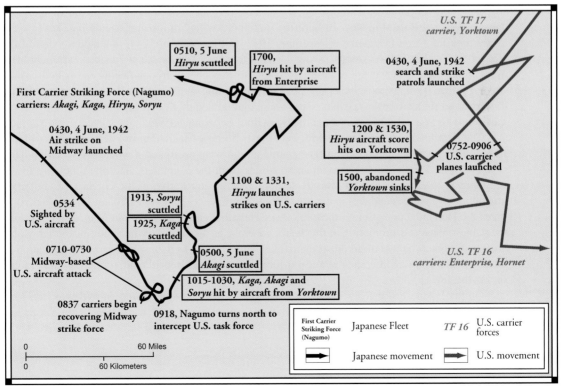

U.S. TF 17
*carrier, Yorktown*

**0510, 5 June**
*Hiryu* scuttled

**1700,**
*Hiryu* hit by aircraft
from Enterprise

**0430, 4 June, 1942**
search and strike
patrols launched

First Carrier Striking Force (Nagumo)
carriers: *Akagi, Kaga, Hiryu, Soryu*

**0430, 4 June, 1942**
Air strike on
Midway launched

**1200 & 1530,**
*Hiryu* aircraft score
hits on Yorktown

**0752-0906**
U.S. carrier
planes launched

**0534**
Sighted by
U.S. aircraft

**1100 & 1331,**
*Hiryu* launches
strikes on U.S. carriers

**1500, abandoned**
*Yorktown* sinks

**1913, Soryu**
scuttled

**1925, Kaga**
scuttled

**0710-0730**
Midway-based
U.S. aircraft attack

**0500, 5 June**
*Akagi* scuttled

**0837 carriers begin
recovering Midway
strike force**

**1015-1030, Kaga, Akagi and
Soryu hit by aircraft from Yorktown**

**0918, Nagumo turns north to
intercept U.S. task force**

U.S. TF 16
*carriers: Enterprise, Hornet*

| 0 | 60 Miles |
| 0 | 60 Kilometers |

| First Carrier Striking Force (Nagumo) | Japanese Fleet | TF 16 | U.S. carrier forces |
| | Japanese movement | → | U.S. movement |

# 41 | NEW GUINEA

New Guinea, a sparsely inhabited colony of Australia and Holland, was the world's second-largest island, with steamy jungles, malarial swamps, and high mountains. To fight here would be combat hell. But the Japanese wanted to occupy Port Moresby, on the southern coast, in order to extend their defensive perimeter and forestall a counterattack by Australian and American soldiers under Douglas MacArthur, commander of the Southwest Pacific theater. The Allies were determined to prevent that, so combat hell came.

Japan advanced twice in 1942 to take Port Moresby; first around Milne Bay by water, and then from Buna on the northern coast across the Owen Stanley Range via the narrow, slippery Kokoda Trail. The Australians (aided by ULTRA) beat back the Milne Bay initiative handily enough. But the Japanese poured thousands of troops into the Kokoda effort, pushed the Australian defenders back, and approached Port Moresby in strength by September. Here they stopped, desperately short of ammunition and food and drained of reinforcements by Tokyo's decision to reinforce Guadalcanal. MacArthur ordered a counterattack by Australian and American troops that regained Kokoda and chased the disorganized Japanese back toward Buna. But the dreadful conditions began to tell on the Allies, whose advance stalled despite reinforcements by air and sea. The entire campaign would have been in jeopardy except that the Japanese, who had received no supplies for weeks, were in worse shape—starving, vomiting blood, without guns, and using the bodies of their own dead for cover. By December the Japanese had lost 12,000 dead from combat, disease, or starvation; the rest simply collapsed, too weak to resist. The Allies suffered 3,000 dead and a staggering 18,000 casualties from malaria.

MacArthur now ordered an advance toward the Japanese garrisons at Lae and Salamaua, which Japan, not wanting to lose here after losing at Guadalcanal, had fortified. It took a year of hard fighting, including amphibious landings and air strikes, and the reduction and isolation of the huge Japanese base at Rabaul in New Britain (the first "bracketing" of a major enemy base) before the Allies took the Huon Peninsula in December 1943. In the spring of 1944, in a land version of the Rabaul bracketing, Allied troops (using ULTRA guidance) bypassed a Japanese stronghold at Wewak and landed far up the coast at Hollandia to trap enemy troops fleeing the Allied coastal drive. Further landings took more key positions, including the Vogelkop Peninsula in July 1944. This marked the end of the terrible island campaign, although 13,000 Japanese from the Wewak garrison withdrew into the interior and held out until September 1945.

The New Guinea campaign went forward partly because MacArthur insisted, over Navy objections, on his own theater command. The campaign did what he argued it would—protect the flank of the Central Pacific drive, draw Japanese forces from the Solomons, and open the way to the Philippines. MacArthur proved himself an able general, innovative in the conduct of combined amphibious operations and deft in the use of local intelligence. Historian William Manchester compares the Hollandia operation to the exploits of Hannibal and Napoleon. But MacArthur was also the vainest, most self-promoting of this war's generals, as disdainful of the conditions in which his soldiers fought as he was of his Australian allies. The Australians themselves earned a reputation as deadly soldiers, giving little quarter and expecting none in the "stench, mud, rottenness and gloom" of this theater.

On the Japanese side, New Guinea revealed the costs of trying to hold an overextended perimeter. The fact that Japanese soldiers were starving as early as 1942 was ominous for the fate of the Japanese empire.

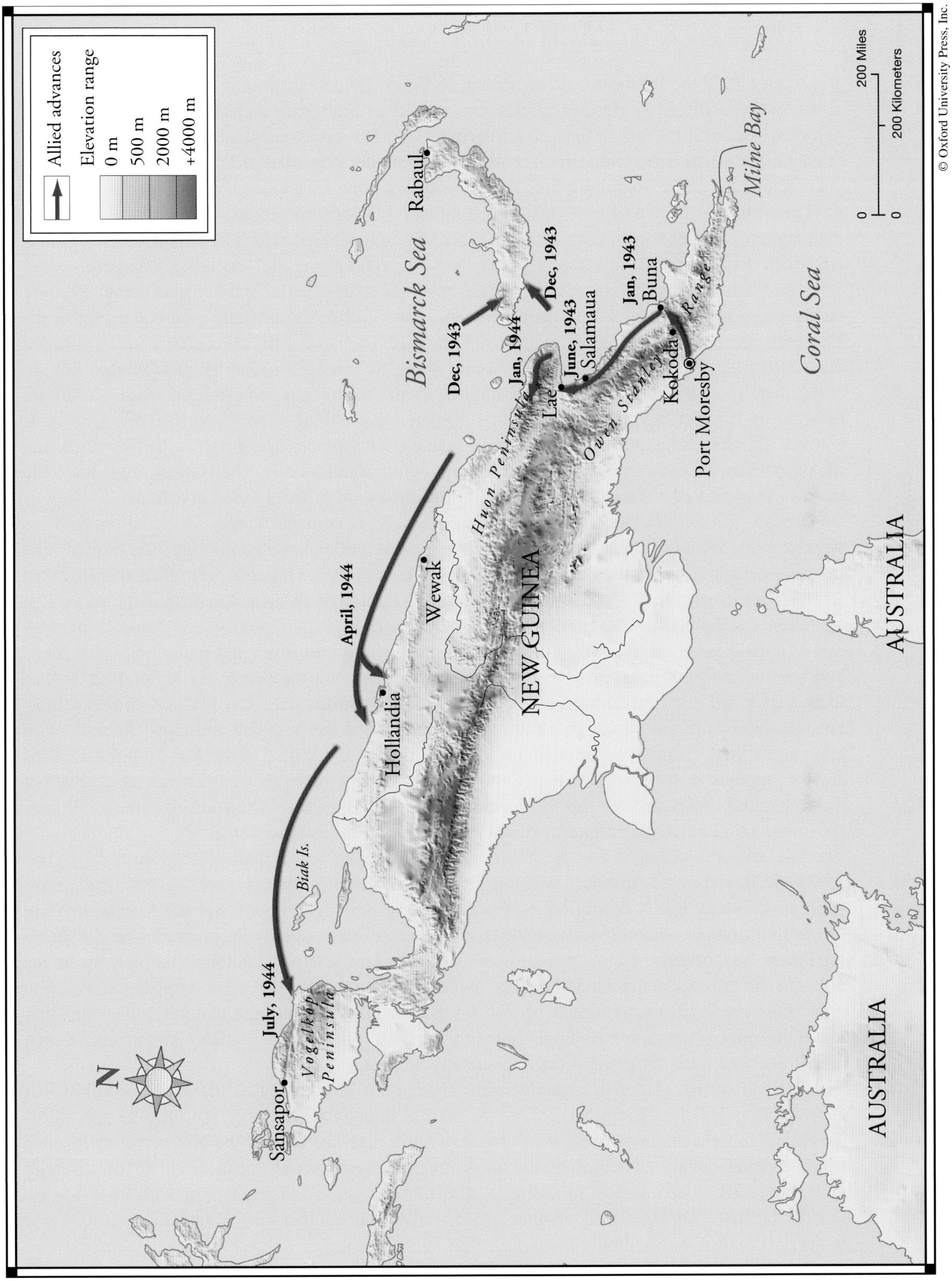

N

Allied advances

Elevation range

0 m
500 m
2000 m
+4000 m

200 Miles
200 Kilometers
0
0

Bismarck Sea

Rabaul

Dec, 1943

Dec, 1943

Jan, 1944

Dec, 1943

Lae

June, 1943
Salamaua

Jan, 1943
Buna

Jan, 1943
Kokoda

Owen Stanley Range

Milne Bay

Port Moresby

Coral Sea

Huon Peninsula

April, 1944

Wewak

NEW GUINEA

AUSTRALIA

Hollandia

Biak Is.

July, 1944

Sansapor

Vogelkop Peninsula

AUSTRALIA

# 42 THE CENTRAL PACIFIC DRIVE

In August 1942 the Japanese built an airstrip on lightly held Guadalcanal in the Solomon chain of the South Pacific. U.S. Marines quickly went ashore to contest the area. The Japanese decided to reinforce; so did the United States. By December, 65,000 men were flailing at each other on the "Canal." The Americans, with army reinforcements, finally prevailed in January and over the next year secured the entire Solomon chain, thereby protecting the New Guinea offensive and the supply lines to Australia. They also encountered three unnerving Japanese combat tactics: jungle fighting, night fighting, and the banzai charge (in which screaming Japanese soldiers hurled themselves against American machine guns)—all responses to superior U.S. firepower, but terrifying nonetheless.

The Solomons operation was protective as much as strategic. The real Central Pacific offensive would begin in the fall of 1943 against Tarawa in the Gilbert Islands and then Kwajalein in the Marshalls, the outer rim of Japan's defensive perimeter. These were flat coral atolls, which afforded defenders little cover, where invaders would have to cross surrounding reefs under fire. In November, Tarawa went badly. The preliminary bombardment was too brief, the landing craft got hung up on the reef, and the marines lost 1,500 men while taking the island. But the Americans learned amphibious lessons. At Kwajalein in January, navy planes and guns crushed the atoll, and the marines (with army support) went ashore on better landing craft. The United States lost only half as many men as at Tarawa. Japan lost 10,000, almost all of them killed in action.

Ahead, 1,500 miles closer to Japan, loomed Saipan, Guam, and Tinian—the Marianas. These were volcanic islands with hills, cliffs, and caves where the Japanese could hide their artillery and machine guns and where they would fight fiercely because the Marianas were their empire's last Central Pacific bastion. So, too, would the Americans fight fiercely, as was evident in the size of the operation: hundreds of ships, 1,000 planes, 250,000 men.

The main target was Saipan, with 40,000 defenders dug into caves and spider holes that shells and bombs could not penetrate. On June 15 the Americans hit the beach. By nightfall 20,000 of them were piled into a beachhead a mile deep. Here they faltered against Japanese artillery, mortars, machine guns, and tanks. But more Americans landed the next day and more the next, with close air support, flame throwers, and artillery. By June 23 the United States had captured airstrips and strongholds in the south of the island and launched a drive to clear all resistance. Mount Tapotchau fell two days later and the northern tip a week after that. The end came on July 9 after the failure of a last desperate banzai charge, the largest of the Pacific war.

The conquest of Saipan cost the Americans 17,000 casualties, including 3,500 dead. Japan had 39,000 dead, victims of American weapons, inadequate supplies (disease and starvation were rampant, as at Buna), and a deadly code of honor: soldiers of the emperor did not surrender. They fought to the end or committed suicide; they blew themselves up, beheaded comrades before shooting themselves, or drowned themselves in the surf. The Japanese naval commander blew his brains out, and the army commander fell on his sword. Unlike previous Japanese outposts, Saipan had many Japanese civilians, thousands of whom killed themselves and their children rather than dishonor the emperor or submit to the ravages of what they called "hairy mongrel Americans." Guam and Tinian were little different, though less costly in lives.

The fall of the Marianas wrought many changes. It brought down the hard-line cabinet of General Tojo Hideki, though his successor proved equally unyielding. By October the B29s, America's biggest bombers, were rumbling down the runways toward the Home Islands. And it changed American attitudes. Among the brass arose a conviction that Japan would never surrender and would have to be invaded. In the ranks, already segregated and prone to racism, arose a sense that the Japanese were inhuman, another species rather than another race. Saipan helped turn a war to the death into a war without mercy.

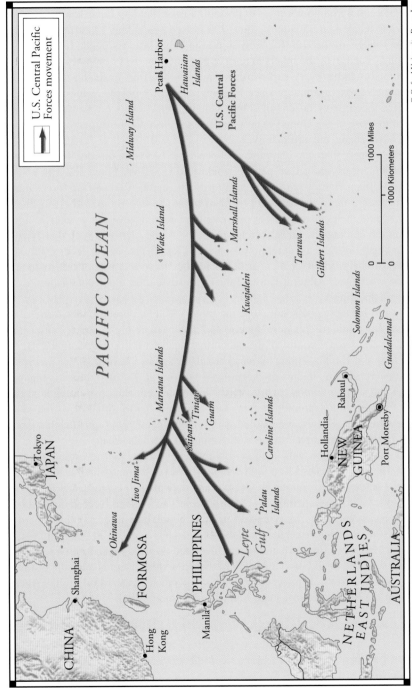

# 43 | THE BATTLE OF LEYTE GULF

MacArthur proposed to retake the Philippines in the fall of 1944 by landing troops at Leyte in the central Philippines prior to invading Luzon, held by Japan since early 1942. To do so, the Americans readied an armada of some 700 vessels, including 32 carriers with 1,400 planes, and 175,000 soldiers of the U.S. 6th Army to hit the Leyte beaches. Japan had 60,000 troops and land-based planes on Leyte and others in reserve elsewhere in the Philippines. Equally important, Tokyo had decided to throw every surviving warship into an effort to shatter the invasion fleet. This was a desperate move. Encounters since Midway, especially off the Solomons and the Marianas, had cost the Imperial navy dozens of ships, including most of its big carriers; Japanese shipyards, in contrast to those of the United States, could not replace them. But enough remained to trigger the largest naval engagement in history.

The Japanese plan was complex, as it needed to be to win this one-sided confrontation. A force of 4 carriers, nearly devoid of planes, would lure U.S. Task Force 38, with 16 big carriers under Admiral William Halsey, northward away from the battle. Two surface forces marshalling 60 warships, including the giant battleships *Musashi* and *Yamato* (both with 18-inch guns and massive armor), would then converge from opposite directions against the weaker 7th Fleet, charged with covering the landings. Launched October 23, 1944, the plan was temporarily successful. Halsey, eager to crush Japanese naval air power once and for all, chased the decoys, although not before his aircraft, with help from U.S. submarines, sank the *Musashi,* a part of the group approaching Leyte from the west under Admiral Kurita Takeo. (*Musashi* took hits from 17 bombs and 19 torpedoes before disappearing.)

But the Japanese could not close the trap. A 7th Fleet group under Admiral Jessie Oldendorf detected the southern Japanese pincer and launched a night attack with surface ships only. Oldendorf destroyed virtually all the oncoming Japanese ships, including the flagship and its admiral, by "crossing the T"—lining his ships broadside against the head of the enemy column, a maneuver that every admiral dreams of executing. To the north, Kurita did better, engaging an arm of the 7th Fleet and sinking several escort carriers and destroyers and positioning himself to wreak havoc on the 7th Fleet. At this point, however, Kurita became fearful of Halsey's return and unexpectedly withdrew his fleet. Halsey, bombarded with radio signals urging his immediate return, showed up, but not in time to participate in the battle or cut off Kurita's escape.

The Battle of Leyte Gulf, though only three days long, was nevertheless a crushing American victory. The United States lost 6 light warships, 200 planes, and 3,000 dead; Japan, however, lost 4 carriers, 3 battleships, 6 cruisers, 12 destroyers, more than 300 planes, and 10,000 pilots and sailors. After Leyte Gulf, the Imperial navy ceased to exist as a viable force. This cleared the way for the invasion and occupation of Leyte and Luzon, although only after months of hard fighting and at a cost of 50,000 American casualties and 400,000 Japanese dead; 100,000 Filipino civilians also died, mostly in Manila, victims of American artillery and frenzied Japanese in a scene reminiscent of the fall of Berlin. And the Filipino Resistance emerged to play a significant supporting role, particularly in the southern islands. Despite communist involvement, MacArthur, unlike American generals in Europe or the British in Burma and Malaya, welcomed its help.

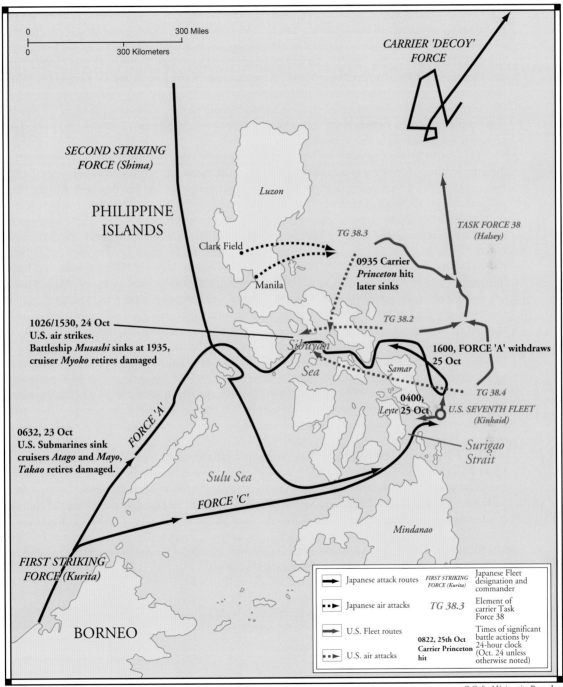

CARRIER 'DECOY' FORCE

SECOND STRIKING FORCE (Shima)

PHILIPPINE ISLANDS

Luzon

Clark Field

Manila

TG 38.3

TASK FORCE 38 (Halsey)

0935 Carrier *Princeton* hit; later sinks

1026/1530, 24 Oct U.S. air strikes. Battleship *Musashi* sinks at 1935, cruiser *Myoko* retires damaged

TG 38.2

*Sibuyan* *Sea*

1600, FORCE 'A' withdraws 25 Oct

Samar

FORCE 'A'

0400, *Leyte* 25 Oct

TG 38.4

U.S. SEVENTH FLEET (Kinkaid)

0632, 23 Oct U.S. Submarines sink cruisers *Atago* and *Mayo*, *Takao* retires damaged.

*Surigao Strait*

*Sulu Sea*

FORCE 'C'

Mindanao

FIRST STRIKING FORCE (Kurita)

BORNEO

| | | |
|---|---|---|
| Japanese attack routes | *FIRST STRIKING FORCE (Kurita)* | Japanese Fleet designation and commander |
| Japanese air attacks | *TG 38.3* | Element of carrier Task Force 38 |
| U.S. Fleet routes | | Times of significant battle actions by 24-hour clock (Oct. 24 unless otherwise noted) |
| U.S. air attacks | **0822, 25th Oct Carrier Princeton hit** | |

0 300 Miles
0 300 Kilometers

© Oxford University Press, Inc.

# 44 | THE STARVATION OF THE HOME ISLANDS

Wartime Japan, like Britain, was a maritime empire dependent on its sea-lanes for prosperity and strength. The Home Islands produced almost no iron or phosphate ore, bauxite, lead or tin, crude oil or rubber, all critical to war production. Imperial expansion guaranteed access to most of these, but they still had to be shipped to Japan proper or to the fighting fronts, as did most of the main food staple, rice. The supply lines to Malaya and the Dutch East Indies were particularly vital, and they were 3,000 miles long. Wartime increases in production in Japan and the empire (rice from Korea and Burma, for instance) made merchant shipping all the more important and the empire all the more vulnerable—doubly so given the extended nature of the defensive perimeter. There were also far too few cargo vessels at any given time, a reflection of the Imperial navy's bias toward the climactic battle as well as its expectation of a short war.

The United States responded as Germany did against Britain, by making war on Japanese shipping. Its weapon of choice was the fleet submarine, which carried 24 torpedoes, could cruise 10,000 miles, and had air conditioning (a godsend when temperatures reached 120 degrees). But the campaign took time to mount. There were only 60 submarines on patrol in 1942, their defective torpedoes often missed the target or failed to explode, and the bases in Hawaii and Australia were too far away. At 20 surface knots, a sub needed 3 weeks to reach the main shipping lanes and 3 weeks to get back. With stores for 55 days, that left just 2 weeks to hunt, far less time than the Nazi U-boats had in the Atlantic. Moving the Hawaii base to Midway helped, as did 30 more subs and better torpedoes. In 1943 American subs sank 300 Japanese merchant ships totaling over 1 million tons.

But the tide truly turned in 1944. American subs could now operate from the Marianas, cutting the round-trip time in half. There were more of them, and they carried not only electric torpedoes that left no wake but radar to protect against Japanese planes. Information from radio decryptions on merchant routes and schedules also helped. U.S. submarines sank 300,000 tons of shipping in October 1944 alone and nearly 3 million for the year. Japanese antisubmarine warfare, undermined by the doctrine of the offensive, was largely ineffectual. By 1945 Japanese merchant vessels were operating mostly in the Sea of Japan at night. Altogether, American subs sank nearly 5 million tons of Imperial shipping plus numerous warships, including a battleship and eight carriers. There were more losses, perhaps 2 million tons, from mines and from direct air strikes as the Pacific fleet closed in on the Home Islands.

The toll on Japan was enormous. War production, which was never sufficient, all but collapsed for lack of materials. From 1944 to 1945, Japanese war production went from 250 warships to 50, from 400 tanks to 140, and from 3,600 fieldpieces to 1,600. Petroleum distillates were down to mere barrels by late spring. Food was running out; Korea doubled its rice production during the war, but the Japanese took most of this and still had to resort in the end to tofu, previously disdained as poverty fare. By summer 1945 average caloric consumption by Japanese servicemen and civilians was below the level needed to sustain life. Not for nothing did the United States call the final phase of the supply interdiction campaign "Operation Starvation."

PACIFIC
OCEAN

U.S.S.R.

JAPAN

KOREA

CHINA

BURMA

INDO-
CHINA

MALAYA

FORMOSA

PHILIPPINES

Marianas

NEW
GUINEA

Solomon
Islands

NETHERLANDS
EAST INDIES

Main areas of Japanese
ship losses 1944

Main areas of Japanese
ship losses 1945

Areas of Japanese control
December 1943

0        1000 Miles
0        1000 Kilometers

# 45 | Okinawa

The decision to attack the Philippines and mount B29 strikes from the Marianas meant that the United States would not have sufficient troops, ships, and bombers to invade Formosa as originally planned. Washington therefore selected new targets: Iwo Jima on the southern end of the Bonin Island chain 700 miles from Tokyo and Okinawa in the Ryukyus near Kyúshú, southernmost of the Home Islands. Iwo, on the path from the Marianas, would serve as a safe harbor for crippled bombers and a takeoff point for fighter escorts. Okinawa, on the path from Luzon, would be the main staging area for the invasion of Japan. Iwo was tiny, 5 miles by 2 miles, and might require comparatively few U.S. troops to subdue. Okinawa was bigger, 60 miles by 15 miles, but smaller than Formosa.

The Iwo Jima landings began February 19 after American planes and ships bombarded the bleak, sulfurous, waterless island. But the 23,000 defenders had dug deep fortifications into Mount Suribachi and elsewhere, where they waited out the bombardment, let the Americans land, and then opened fire. The United States employed three marine divisions in the assault, which was expected to last a few days and to cost 10,000 casualties. It took a month and 25,000 casualties, including 7,000 dead marines. Mop-up troops eventually counted over 21,000 Japanese bodies; 1,000 Japanese surrendered, most of them wounded or weak from disease.

Iwo Jima was ghastly, but Okinawa was worse. Here the Japanese had 130,000 troops, well supplied and dug in, particularly at Sugar Loaf Hill and other spots below the heavily defended Shuri Line, which incorporated ancient thick-walled Shuri Castle and a large Okinawan burial ground. Okinawa also had 400,000 civilians. The United States countered with 180,000 soldiers and marines and at least that many supporting troops, 100 warships (including some British) with aircraft, and 1,000 other craft. Again, there was much bombardment to little effect. U.S. troops struck the undefended beaches on Easter Sunday, April 1. By day's end 50,000 were ashore, with few losses. Marines took the northern part of the island fairly quickly. Army units moving south bogged down against withering fire, as did marine reinforcements. Heavy rain obscured air targets and increased the misery. Not until May 18 did the Americans breach the Shuri Line. Not until June 21 did they declare Okinawa secure. The Japanese paid for this sacrificial defense with 100,000 dead, although nearly 10,000 surrendered, something not seen before. More than 140,000 civilians died, many by suicide. The United States suffered 76,000 casualties, including 21,000 dead.

Among the U.S. dead were 5,000 sailors, the targets of suicide kamikaze planes designed to disrupt the U.S. invasion and make it vulnerable to surface attacks. First employed at Leyte Gulf, kamikaze ("divine wind") were common by early 1945 because they did not require skilled pilots or full tanks of gasoline, neither any longer available. At Okinawa kamikaze pilots sank 30 vessels and damaged hundreds of others. Most of the vessels were small, but 5 carriers were hit. Kamikaze were the banzai charges of the air, terrifying and demoralizing but wasteful. The Americans pressed on despite their casualties.

Iwo Jima and Okinawa tested the doctrine of amphibious warfare, the landing of troops on enemy territory by sea. Amphibious warfare's chief proponent was the U.S. Marine Corps, a pioneer in the development of amphibious landing craft, communications, and air and sea support. MacArthur, whose army forces used amphibious landings with increasing frequency, was skeptical of assaulting the Japanese-held islands, which offered no room for maneuver and would produce disproportionate losses. He was right about the losses, but the casualties rose mainly when the Japanese stopped contesting the beaches and dug into the islands' interior to die. This was ground, not amphibious, combat, more like Stalingrad than Tarawa. Advanced amphibious operations were one of the major innovations of the war, along with strategic bombing and armored warfare. For all the losses, nowhere did the Allied amphibious operations fail.

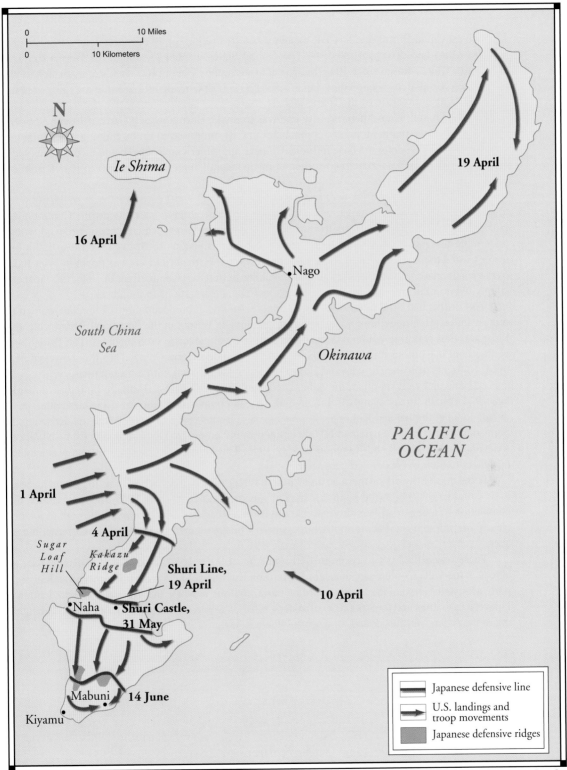

N

0 ___ 10 Miles
0 ___ 10 Kilometers

*Ie Shima*

**16 April**

**19 April**

•Nago

*South China Sea*

*Okinawa*

**1 April**

**4 April**

*Sugar Loaf Hill*

*Kakazu Ridge*

**Shuri Line, 19 April**

•Naha  • **Shuri Castle, 31 May**

**10 April**

*PACIFIC OCEAN*

Mabuni•  • **14 June**

Kiyamu•

| | Japanese defensive line |
| --- | --- |
| → | U.S. landings and troop movements |
| ▓ | Japanese defensive ridges |

The vast China-Burma-India (CBI) theater was a frustration for all concerned, not least because the Allies had divergent interests. The United States wanted to rebuild the Burma Road to Nationalist China, closed since 1942, and use it to strengthen Chiang Kai-shek's army, which might retake the coastal areas occupied by Japan since 1938. East China could become a staging area for B29 raids and an invasion of the Home Islands.

For the United States, then, priority one was to retake Burma, which General Joseph Stilwell, an old China hand and the top U.S. commander in CBI, proposed to do by training and equipping several Chinese divisions at a base in India. Chinese and American troops would then invade North Burma. Priority two was to help construct an independent China strong enough to play a stabilizing role in postwar Asia.

Although Chiang Kai-shek very much wanted American Lend-Lease assistance, he did not want to waste his troops fighting Japan when he was going to need them later against the Communists. Nor did he trust Stilwell's efforts to reform China's corrupt army, which Chiang believed would undermine his authority in Chungking. He sent several divisions to Stilwell's base in India but never trusted them and did little else except contest for U.S. materiel as it was flown in from India over the Himalayas. When the B29 runs from China started to have an effect in 1944, the Japanese simply overran the airfields, leaving Chiang's ineffectual formations in the dust.

The British had little interest in these Chinese-American preoccupations. Churchill wanted to protect India, seething with nationalist unrest, and invade Burma in the direction of Mandalay and Rangoon, thus restoring colonial control and setting up an advance on Singapore. The British had neither faith in Chinese abilities nor commitment to an independent China. They did, however, permit U.S. flights over the Himalayan "Hump" and provide Stilwell with a training base.

Capable and well supplied, the Allies predictably moved against Burma in both directions. In late 1944 British forces of mostly Indian and African composition stopped a Japanese attempt to invade India at Imphal and Kohima and sent Japanese troops reeling back through the dense jungle highlands. The Japanese sustained 60,000 casualties, including 13,000 dead, many from starvation. Mandalay fell in March and Rangoon in May 1945. The Japanese collapse in Burma was another testament to their overextended perimeter.

In the north Stilwell's American and Chinese forces took Myitkyina, with its important airfield, in the summer of 1944 as the battle for Imphal was raging, and in early 1945 Stilwell oversaw the completion of a new road from Ledo to the old Burma Road. By now, however, the path to victory clearly lay through the Pacific, not China, where Chiang seemed as ineffectual and unwilling as ever.

There was a final act to come in CBI. On August 9 the U.S.S.R. declared war on Japan, as agreed at the Yalta Conference, and sent 1.5 million Russian soldiers with full armored and air support against the Kwantung Army in Manchuria. Within a week the Russians inflicted 80,000 Japanese casualties and took 600,000 prisoners, most of whom were sent to labor camps. The fighting in the Asian war thus ended, in a sense, where it began.

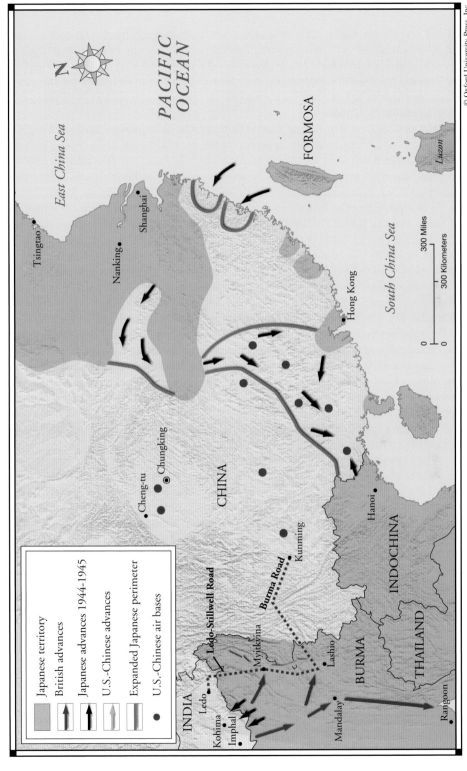

# 47 | THE AIR WAR

The air war on Japan had two components, both dictated by the tyranny of vast distance. Component one was naval warfare centered on the aircraft carrier, the floating airstrip that brought planes within range of their target. Initially the prize for carrier aircraft excellence went to the Imperial Navy's nimble Mitsubishi Zero, which had a ceiling of 39,000 feet and a range of 1,900 miles, an excellent fighter plane for the vast Pacific theater. Japan built 11,000 Zeros, and until 1943 their superiority was manifest.

But the Zero was fragile and needed skilled pilots to exploit its agility. The U.S. Navy's F6 Hellcat and F4 Corsair, available in the thousands by 1943, were stodgier but faster and tougher, and they downed Zeros in large numbers, particularly as Japan lost pilots that its restricted training programs could not adequately replace. In an encounter west of the Marianas in June 1944, Hellcats destroyed 400 Japanese planes (along with their pilots) and three carriers. Books call it the Battle of the Philippine Sea; the Americans called it the "Marianas Turkey Shoot." It virtually eliminated Japanese naval air power. By late 1944 U.S. carrier aircraft were killing Japanese cargo ships across the whole far western Pacific with bombs, torpedoes, and rockets. In the summer of 1945, American carriers closed tightly on the Home Islands and conducted devastating raids on Japanese coastal cities, ranging with impunity through Japanese skies bereft of planes, pilots, and fuel.

Component two was strategic bombing centered on a heavy land-based army bomber, the B29, which could fly at 36,000 feet for 1,500 miles and back at 360 miles per hour with nearly five tons of bombs. The cost for 3,000 B29s was $3 billion—$1 million each—a huge amount in 1940s dollars. Conceived as a precision bomber against Germany, the B29 was deployed by Washington in the Pacific because no other bomber could reach Japan from the available bases.

The first B29 sorties were in mid-1944 from India and, after a grueling flight over the Himalayas, from China. The targets were mainly in the occupied regions—Bangkok, Shanghai, Indochina, Sumatra, Singapore—with some strikes against steelworks and aircraft plants in southern Japan, still barely reachable. But it took six Himalaya "Hump" flights to mount one bombing mission from China, altitude and winds ruined all accuracy, losses were high, and the Chinese airfields were vulnerable to ground attack.

The campaign therefore underwent two changes. First, the Marianas, now in U.S. hands, became the main base, bringing central Japan within range. Second, since losses remained high (mostly from stalled engines and in-flight collisions) and accuracy was poor, there was a shift from precision day bombing to low-level night attacks with incendiaries in order to produce firestorms, an easier task in Japan's wooden cities than in Germany. The results were devastating. By June the B29s had destroyed large areas of urban Japan—26 percent of Osaka, 44 percent of Yokohama, 76 percent of Nagoya. The death toll, mostly civilians, was huge. A March 10, 1945, raid burned 40 percent of Tokyo and killed over 80,000 people, and Tokyo suffered additional mass bomber attacks.

There was concern in high American circles about this hammering of civilians, but General Curtis LeMay, the campaign commander, argued that bombing might force a surrender, which would make an invasion unnecessary and save American lives, and that Japan's production facilities were scattered in civilian areas, so to get at industries, civilians had to be killed. Bombing, if it forced a surrender, might even prevent the mass starvation threatened by the submarine campaign. And after the high casualties at Saipan and elsewhere, Americans did not much care what happened to the Japanese. The sooner the war ended, the better, whatever the rain of death from the skies. The results were appalling, what historians Guy Wint and Peter Calvocoressi call "deliberate, indiscriminate mass murder."

Still Japan would not surrender, so there was more death to come.

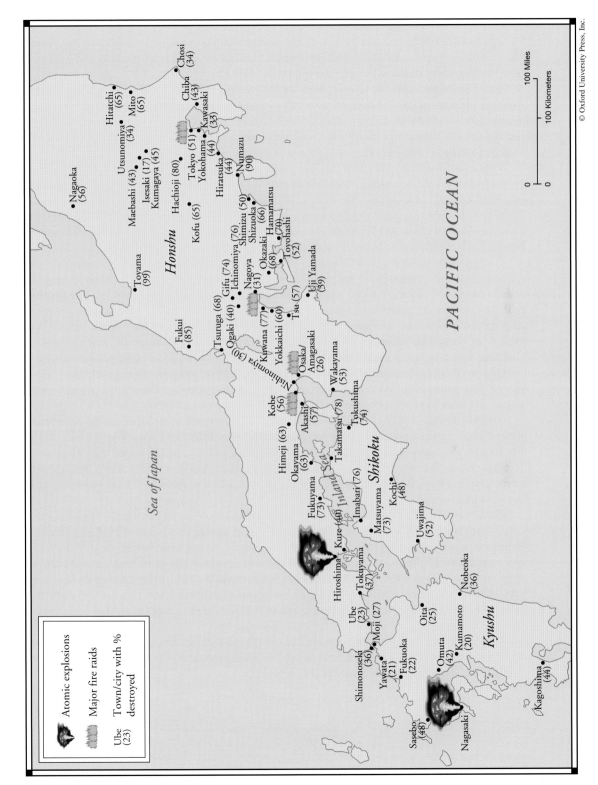

Atomic explosions

Major fire raids

Ube
(23)    Town/city with % destroyed

*Sea of Japan*

*Honshu*

Nagaoka
(56)

Toyama
(99)

Hitatchi
(65)

Utsunomiya
(34)

Mito
(65)

Maebashi (43)
Isesaki (17)
Kumagaya (45)

Hachioji (80)

Kofu (65)

Fukui
(85)

Tsuruga (68)

Gifu (74)

Ogaki (40)

Ichinomiya (76)

Shimizu (50)

Shizuoka
(66)

Nagoya
(31)

Okazaki
(68)

Hamamatsu
(70)

Toyohashi
(52)

Kuwana (77)

Yokkaichi (60)

*Nishinomiya (30)*

Tsu (57)

Uji Yamada
(39)

Chosi (34)

Chiba (43)

Kawasaki
(33)

Tokyo (51)

Yokohama
(44)

Hiratsuka
(44)

Numazu
(90)

Osaka/
Amagasaki
(26)

Kobe
(56)

Akashi
(57)

Himeji (63)

Okayama
(63)

Fukuyama
(73)

Kure (40)

Hiroshima

Tokuyama
(37)

Ube
(23)

Moji (27)

Shimonoseki
(36)

Yawata
(21)

Fukuoka
(22)

Omuta
(42)

Kumamoto
(20)

Oita
(25)

Nobeoka
(36)

Sasebo
(48)

Nagasaki

Kagoshima
(44)

*Kyushu*

Wakayama
(53)

Tokushima
(74)

Takamatsu (78)

Imabari (76)

Matsuyama (73)

Kochi
(48)

Uwajima
(52)

*Shikoku*

*Inland Sea*

*PACIFIC OCEAN*

100 Miles

100 Kilometers

0

0

© Oxford University Press, Inc.

# 48 THE ATOMIC BOMB

The United States helped win the war partly through sheer organization—producing gargantuan quantities of arms, mobilizing and deploying 12 million troops at peak strength, and supplying food, medicine, and clothing to its forces and those of its allies.

But science was critical, too. Fighting at long range required better eyes and ears, hence advances in radar, radio, and decryption. Swift movement demanded faster and more precise calculations, hence electronics. War against cities demanded delivery capacity and destructive power. Heavy bombers and aircraft carriers were such delivery systems, as were the German V1 and V2 rockets; blockbuster bombs and incendiaries provided the destructive power.

Physicists thought by the 1930s that they could release still more explosive energy by splitting the nucleus of the atom, making it possible to produce a weapon so terrible that whatever country possessed it could not lose; they also thought that Germany, formidable in physics despite the exodus of Jewish scientists, might develop such a weapon. In 1939 several physicists, including Albert Einstein, wrote to Roosevelt about the danger. From this came a crash program, the "Manhattan Project," to build an atomic bomb for use in Europe.

Controlled by a handful of Washington officials (Churchill knew, but Vice President Truman did not), the Manhattan Project's headquarters was in Los Alamos, New Mexico, where American, British, and émigré scientists toiled round the clock on the theory and practice of splitting uranium nuclei to fashion a chain-reaction explosion. Facilities in Tennessee and Washington State produced uranium and plutonium, a uranium derivative; facilities in California, New York, and Illinois worked on separation techniques as well as triggering and control materials; and facilities in Michigan and Wisconsin made critical components. By 1944 the Manhattan Project employed 600,000 people at eight major U.S. sites, making it the largest weapons development program in history. The government fed it with the entire uranium output of the Congo, the world's major source, and with so much aluminum that it disrupted construction of B29s.

The Manhattan Project succeeded. On July 16, 1945, the scientists successfully detonated a plutonium device at Alamogordo, New Mexico, and in short order two actual bombs were ready to use. By now the European war was over, but a committee had already developed a list of possible targets in Japan. One was Hiroshima in southern Honshu, with 350,000 inhabitants and scattered war plants; Nagasaki, in northern Kyushu, was smaller but had a steelworks. Both cities had military training facilities.

On August 6, a B29 from the Marianas dropped a uranium bomb on Hiroshima; three days later a plutonium bomb hit Nagasaki. Each had a blast force of thousands of tons of TNT and produced temperatures of a million degrees. Blast and heat together damaged or destroyed most of the buildings in both cities, killed between 100,000 and 140,000 people at Hiroshima and perhaps half that many at Nagasaki, and left tens of thousands injured (some with melted eyeballs or fused lips, some with wounds from thousands of slivers of glass and metal, and others whose skin had slid from their limbs). The bombs also unleashed radiation that took, over the next generation, tens of thousands of additional lives.

On August 14 the emperor broke a deadlock in his cabinet, announced his decision to yield to the Allies, and notified his unbelieving subjects, in an unprecedented public broadcast, that they should cease all their efforts to resist the invaders.

## A. Manhattan Project

WASHINGTON
Hanford •

**Production of plutonium**

CANADA

WISCONSIN
Milwaukee •

**Production of pumps**

MICH.
Detroit •

Chicago •

NEW YORK

New York •

**Production of diffusers**

**Development of gaseous diffusion process for U-235 separation**

Berkeley •

**Development of electromagnetic process for U-235 separation**

ILLINOIS
Decatur •

**Plutonium research program**

**Production of barrier**

Washington ⊙

CALIFORNIA

**Bomb design and assembly**

Los • Alamos

NEW MEXICO

VIRGINIA

TENNESSEE

• Oak Ridge

**Production of U-235**

Alamogordo •

**First nuclear explosion "Trinity" 16 July 1945**

N

| | Component manufacturing |
| | Scientific research |
| | Test site |
| | Uranium/plutonium production |

MEXICO

0        500 Miles
0      500 Kilometers

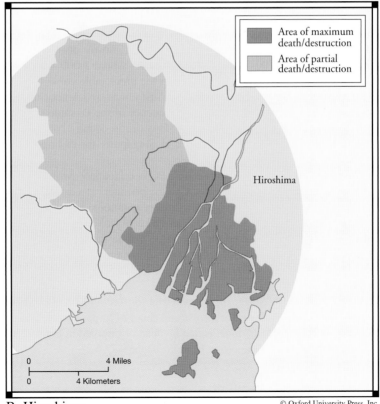

| | Area of maximum death/destruction |
| | Area of partial death/destruction |

Hiroshima

0        4 Miles
0      4 Kilometers

## B. Hiroshima

U.S. troops occupied a devastated Japan. Nearly 3 million Japanese were dead; 5 million wounded, sick, or starving; 9 million homeless. One-third of the national wealth was gone. A country desperately needing to pull together shunned its former soldiers as losers and brutes, its war widows and orphans as "improper," its bombing victims and disabled (especially from the nuclear cities) as tainted. The United States provided less help than in Germany. Huge numbers of Japanese survived for years as prostitutes, on meager foreign aid, or by begging. Production only slowly returned to prewar levels. The occupation formally ended in 1951 when Tokyo renounced its control of Korea and Taiwan, gave the Marianas and other island groups to the United States in trusteeship, and relinquished Sakhalin to Russia. By then the Korean War was in full swing. Prosperity was finally around the corner.

As in Germany, the Americans instituted reforms that they hoped would prevent future aggression. They dissolved the armed forces, broke up industrial conglomerates, redistributed land, and barred 200,000 "undesirables" from government service. A new constitution retained the emperor but gave women the right to vote; guaranteed labor unions, press freedoms, and political party competition; and prohibited all resort to war.

MacArthur, the supreme commander, also arranged a counterpart to the Nuremberg Trials, an International Military Tribunal for the Far East with judges from 11 countries and an American as chief prosecutor. The Tribunal tried 25 Japanese for perpetrating aggression and failing to halt atrocities such as Nanking and convicted them all: 7, including General Tojo Hideki (the former prime minister), were hanged; 16 received life in prison; 2 got lesser sentences. An Indian judge dissented on the grounds that wars of aggression were not crimes in international law, a Filipino criticized the "lenient" sentences, and an Australian opposed the death sentences because Emperor Hirohito, the ultimate authority, was not on trial (MacArthur, having decided that keeping the emperor would make the occupation easier, did not want him tried).

Ten countries conducted their own war crimes trials, mostly dealing with the treatment of POWs and civilians. Some 5,700 Japanese stood trial, of whom 3,000 were convicted and more than 900 were executed. This rate of conviction was the predictable consequence of the harshness of the POW camps, where 27 percent of the British, Australians, and Americans, and probably more of the Asians, died. This was in turn partly a consequence of the Bushido principle that surrender was a disgrace warranting contempt and brutality. Many deaths occurred on work details. More than 12,000 British Commonwealth soldiers captured at Singapore, for example, died constructing a Thai-Burma railway.

Racism played a part, especially with Chinese POWs. Japanese Army Unit 731, charged with developing bacteriological weapons, subjected Chinese prisoners at a camp in Manchuria to plague, cholera, and typhus injections as well as hypothermia, gravitational pressure, and vivisection. Japan used plague germs against Chinese troops and cities and against Soviet soldiers (accidentally killing thousands of its own men) and studied the release of plague fleas as a defense if the Americans invaded the Home Islands. The U.S.S.R. convicted some members of Unit 731 after the war; the United States granted immunity to Unit members in its custody in exchange for confidential access to their records.

Gender, too, played a part. No Japanese stood trial for forcing Koreans, Chinese, and others to serve as "comfort women," sex slaves for the use and abuse of Imperial soldiers. The Japanese army held 200,000 women in its brothels; most ended up dead or crippled in body, mind, or spirit. They received neither compensation nor apology from the Japanese.

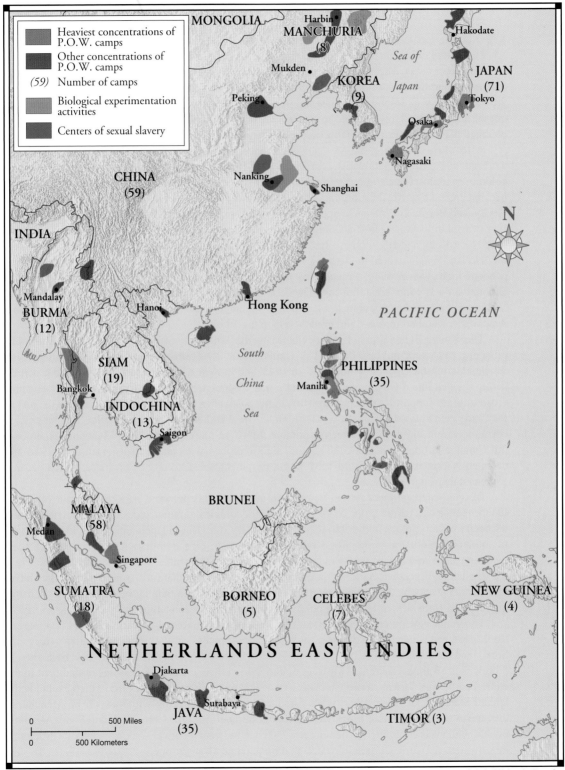

**Heaviest concentrations of P.O.W. camps**

**Other concentrations of P.O.W. camps**

*(59)* **Number of camps**

**Biological experimentation activities**

**Centers of sexual slavery**

MONGOLIA

Harbin
MANCHURIA
(8)
Hakodate

Mukden

Peking

KOREA
(9)

Sea of
Japan

JAPAN
(71)

Tokyo

Osaka

Nagasaki

CHINA
(59)

Nanking

Shanghai

INDIA

N

Mandalay
BURMA
(12)

Hanoi

Hong Kong

PACIFIC OCEAN

SIAM
(19)

Bangkok

South

China

Sea

PHILIPPINES
(35)

Manila

INDOCHINA
(13)

Saigon

MALAYA
(58)

BRUNEI

Medan

Singapore

SUMATRA
(18)

BORNEO
(5)

CELEBES
(7)

NEW GUINEA
(4)

NETHERLANDS EAST INDIES

Djakarta

Surabaya

0         500 Miles

0         500 Kilometers

JAVA
(35)

TIMOR (3)

# 50 INDEPENDENT ASIA

Wartime Japan tried to enlist the peoples of Asia in a race-based pan-Asian front against the Western colonialists, even sponsoring anti-Western (and anti-communist) nationalist movements in some areas. This did not work well anywhere. The Japanese proved no less rapacious and predatory than the Europeans. As a Burmese said, "The British sucked our blood, the Japanese ground our bones." In any case most indigenous independence movements predated Japan's conquests and had their own ideology and social bases. Anti-Japanese resistance movements also emerged that contributed to Japan's defeat and fanned the pro-independence flames.

After years of fighting the Axis powers, France, Holland, and even Britain were ill-positioned to resist this cresting nationalist sentiment. The British mostly did not try, relinquishing their colonies in almost the same order in which they had acquired them centuries before. In 1947 India became free; large Moslem regions then broke away to form Pakistan. Independence came to Ceylon and Burma in 1948 and a decade later to Malaya, though only after Britain, with Malay support, waged bitter war against a Communist insurgency. Of the empire on which the sun never set, only Hong Kong and a few other small places remained.

Holland fought to hold the Dutch East Indies—oil still mattered—but had to recognize an independent Indonesia in 1949. France also fought to hold Indo-China, partly because Vietnamese nationalism was communist, but lost despite U.S. military aid and advisors. Laos, Cambodia, and Vietnam became independent in 1954, although Vietnam would be engulfed in bloody war until the Americans, who had replaced the French, left in the 1970s.

The United States granted independence to the Philippines in 1946 but retained enormous influence and major military bases. The United States also remained influential both in postwar Thailand, after the Japanese withdrawal in 1945, and in Korea, independent as of 1945 but permanently divided into a Communist north and a non-Communist south. In China the Americans provided military support for Chiang Kai-shek in his postwar struggle against the Communists, just as they had given him aid during the war with Japan—and with much the same results. The Nationalist corruption went too deep for effective combat. Mao Tse-tung's armies took Manchuria, then central China, and finally, in 1949, the south, an eerie replay of Japan's expansion in the 1930s. The defeated Nationalists relocated to Taiwan, the former Japanese colony of Formosa, which became a client state of the Americans.

By mid-century there were more than a dozen independent nations instead of three. Independence was hardly utopia: There was much ideological, ethnic, and religious violence; much desperate poverty; much authoritarianism and military rule. But independence brought a reduction in colonial exploitation, relief from the humiliation of foreign domination, and (in some places, including India and Japan) democracy. And India after 1947, China after 1949, and Japan itself—the Big Three of postwar Asia with a quarter of the earth's population—were by and large stable, itself an achievement. Australia played a larger role in East Asia than before, eventually exchanging its racist fortress mentality for a policy of openness and partnership.

The major new power was America, nuclear-armed but perched precariously on a five-legged stool of pacifist Japan, divided Korea, oligarchic Philippines, army-dominated Thailand (formerly Siam), and Chiang's exiles in Taiwan. Even with Australia's support, this was a modest base, though it drew Cold War America into two wars that together killed as many Americans as had died in the entire Pacific war. Taiwan, moreover, was a poor substitute for mainland China, which excluded the United States for decades. The Soviets fared no better there; having withdrawn from Manchuria, they never got back. Neither the Soviets nor the Americans (nor the Chinese) found South Asia hospitable. India was committed to democracy, Pakistan to Islam. Postwar Asia, whatever its problems, thus avoided the "Iron Curtain" division that plagued postwar Europe.

**Colonial Affiliations before 1945**

U.S. territory
British territory
Dutch territory
French territory
Independent before 1945
Japanese territory
Russian territory
⊗ Japanese-supported Anti-colonial movements
⊗ Radical Anti-Japanese resistance movments

RUSSIA

AFGHANISTAN

CHINA

KOREA (divided 1945)

JAPAN

PACIFIC OCEAN

PAKISTAN 1947

NEPAL

LAOS 1954

TAIWAN (to China, 1945)

INDIA 1947

BURMA 1948

THAILAND

CAMBODIA 1954

VIETNAM (divided 1954)

PHILIPPINES 1946

CEYLON 1948

MALAYA 1957

INDIAN OCEAN

INDONESIA 1949

0          1000 Miles
0          1000 Kilometers

AUSTRALIA

# INDEX